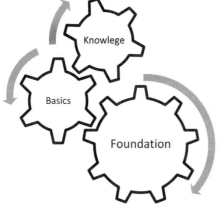

Teradata 14
Basics

An Authorized Teradata Certified Professional Program Study Guide

Exam TE0-141

First Edition

ISBN 978-0-9830242-9-3
Printed by Cerulium Corporation

Stephen Wilmes
Eric Rivard

Copyright

Trademarks

Special Acknowledgement

A special thank you to the following individuals that contributed to the Study Guide content: Marta Beckett, Barbara Christjohn, Susan Hahn, Julie Huber, and Larry Rex.

About the Author - Steve Wilmes

Steve Wilmes founded Cerulium Corporation in 2007. As Chief Executive Officer, his goal is to establish Cerulium as a premier data warehousing Technology Company. Cerulium's strategic growth is globally focused on six lines of business including education, consulting, BI solutions, productivity tools, application integration and assessment services. These lines of business have been highly successful by utilizing strategic data warehousing solutions provided by Teradata that spans across the consumer, and commercial markets.

Mr. Wilmes has over 20 years of experience in the computer industry and is known to be a detail-oriented, results-focused leader. He is an internationally recognized expert in several aspects of data warehousing including hardware, software, SQL, operating systems, implementation, data integration, database administration, and BI solutions.

Mr. Wilmes earned a bachelor's degree in business administration and economics in 1994 from Augsburg College and he is also a Teradata Certified Master.

Mr. Wilmes resides just outside of Columbia, South Carolina, with his wife, Becky. He has been involved with numerous civic, educational, and business organizations throughout his career. Some of his more recent associations include working with the Richland County Sheriff's Department – Region 4 Community Member, and volunteer for local organizations where he shares his technical expertise.

About the Author - Eric Rivard

Eric Rivard is the COO and Vice President of Cerulium Corporation, and is responsible for consulting and product development operations. Mr. Rivard has substantial industry experience across the telecommunications, retail, and healthcare industries, and has consulted at many Fortune 500 companies. His in-depth knowledge of the Teradata platform has enabled him to design and develop customized Teradata applications. He has worked with some of the largest data warehouses in the world, providing unique software solutions and solving complex business problems.

Mr. Rivard dedicated the bulk of his career to the pursuit of data heterogeneity. Outside of this Teradata expertise, he worked extensively with a variety of database platforms, and developed software products that integrate across the different RDBMS systems. He is an experienced Microsoft .NET developer, which has enabled him to use Microsoft's best-in-class development tools as a foundation for Cerulium Corporation's data warehouse applications.

Mr. Rivard resides just outside of Atlanta, Georgia, with his wife, Susana, and their three children. Outside of his professional career, he is actively involved in many community activities. In addition, he serves on the Advisory Board for the Management Information Systems (MIS) program at his alma mater, the Terry College of Business at the University of Georgia, where he earned his Bachelor of Business Administration in MIS and International Business.

Table of Contents

The Teradata Certified Professional Program

Pursue Teradata Certification with Confidence™

The Teradata Certified Professional Program (TCPP), launched in 1999, develops and manages Teradata's premier, and only, certification testing program. Teradata authorized training and proctored exams, available globally to customers, partners, associates, and students, are instrumental in establishing an industry-standard measure of technical competence for IT professionals using Teradata technology. Recognized as a leader in Data Warehouse RDBMS technology and valued by major global companies using Teradata, more than 57,000 Teradata Certifications have been awarded.

The new Teradata 14 Certification Track consists of seven exams that combine for achievement of six certifications and provides a logical progression for specific job roles. Starting with the core Teradata 14 Certified Professional credential, individuals have an opportunity to demonstrate knowledge by achieving Certification as a Technical Specialist, Database Administrator, Solutions Developer, Enterprise Architect, and the most prestigious Teradata Certification – Teradata 14 Certified Master.

The purpose of this Certification Exam Study Guide is to assist you with your goal to become Teradata Certified. This Guide will provide focused content areas, high level explanations around the key areas of focus, and help you to determine areas of further study prior to sitting for the Teradata Certification examination.

Although the Exam Study Guide will assist you in exam preparation, you must be knowledgeable of the subject areas in order to pass the exam. This Guide is intended for individuals who have completed the recommended training and have the recommended amount of Teradata experience. **We do not guarantee that you will pass the exam simply by reading the Exam Study Guide.** Only hard work, hands-on experience, and a positive attitude will help you to achieve exam success. We wish you the very best of luck!

> *"When hiring, I always look for Teradata Certified Professionals. Not only does it provide me a good understanding of a candidate's knowledge level, it also shows a commitment to continuous learning and self-improvement. That's a great trait to have in every employee and the Teradata Certified Professional Program makes it easy to recognize."*
>
> *Teradata Certified Master, Insurance Industry*

The flowchart and matrix below are designed to help you define a path to the knowledge, skills, and experience needed to achieve Teradata 14 Certifications.

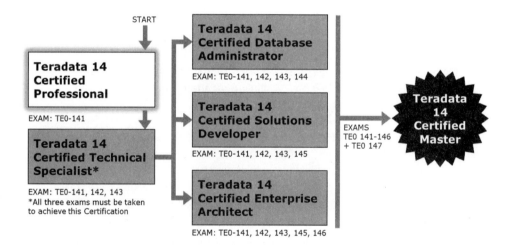

Your Teradata 14 Certification Upgrade Roadmap

Teradata 12 Certified candidates, in good standing, are eligible to take the *Teradata 14 Bridge from Teradata 12 Exam (TE0-14B)*. The Bridge exam is a hybrid of all three (3) Teradata baseline Certification exams, and covers content changes to Teradata Basics, Teradata SQL and Teradata Physical Design & Implementation exams.

A passed exam result on the Bridge exam will yield the *Teradata 14 Certified Technical Specialist* designation. A candidate may then continue on the Teradata 14 track until achieving the desired Certification level.

Teradata 14 Certifications

Teradata 14 Certified Professional

Exams Required:
- TE0-141 – Teradata 14 Basics

Must be passed before continuing on certification path

Recommended Teradata Experience:
6-12 months

Recommended Preparation Courses:
- Introduction to the Teradata Database

Teradata 14 Certified Technical Specialist

Exams Required:
- TE0-141 – Teradata 14 Basics
- TE0-142 – Teradata 14 SQL
- TE0-143 – Teradata 14 Physical Design and Implementation

3 Exams to be passed in sequential order

Recommended Teradata Experience:
1-2 years

Recommended Preparation Courses:
- Introduction to the Teradata Database
- Teradata SQL
- Advanced Teradata SQL
- Physical Database Design
- Physical Database Tuning

Teradata 14 Certified Database Administrator

Exams Required:
- TE0-141 – Teradata 14 Basics
- TE0-142 – Teradata 14 SQL
- TE0-143 – Teradata 14 Physical Design and Implementation
- TE0-144 – Teradata 14 Database Administration

4 Exams to be passed in sequential order

Recommended Teradata Experience:
2-3 years

Recommended Preparation Courses:
- Introduction to the Teradata Database
- Teradata SQL
- Advanced Teradata SQL
- Physical Database Design
- Physical Database Tuning
- Teradata Application Utilities
- Teradata Parallel Transporter
- Teradata Warehouse Management
- Teradata Warehouse Administration

Teradata 14 Certified Solutions Developer

Exams Required:
- TE0-141 – Teradata 14 Basics
- TE0-142 – Teradata 14 SQL
- TE0-143 – Teradata 14 Physical Design and Implementation
- TE0-145 – Teradata 14 Solutions Development

4 Exams to be passed in sequential order

Recommended Teradata Experience:
2-3 years

Recommended Preparation Courses:
- Introduction to the Teradata Database
- Teradata SQL
- Advanced Teradata SQL
- Physical Database Design
- Physical Database Tuning
- Teradata Application Utilities
- Teradata Parallel Transporter
- Teradata Application Design and Development

Teradata 14 Certified Enterprise Architect

Exams Required:
- TE0-141 – Teradata 14 Basics
- TE0-142 – Teradata 14 SQL
- TE0-143 – Teradata 14 Physical Design and Implementation
- TE0-145 – Teradata 14 Solutions Development
- TE0-146 – Teradata 14 Enterprise Architecture

5 Exams to be passed in sequential order

Recommended Teradata Experience:
2-3 years

Recommended Preparation Courses:

- Introduction to the Teradata Database
- Teradata SQL
- Advanced Teradata SQL
- Physical Database Design
- Physical Database Tuning
- Teradata Application Utilities
- Teradata Parallel Transporter
- Teradata Warehouse Management
- Teradata Warehouse Administration
- Teradata Application Design and Development

Teradata 14 Certified Master*

Exams Required:
- TE0-141 - TE0-146: Successful completion of all exams **PLUS:**
- TE0-147 – Teradata 14 Comprehensive Mastery Exam

7 Exams to be passed in sequential order

*Path for Teradata 12 Certified Masters
- TE0-147 – Teradata 14 Comprehensive Mastery Exam

Recommended Teradata Experience:
A minimum 5 years practical hands-on experience is highly recommended

Recommended Preparation Courses:
- Introduction to the Teradata Database
- Teradata SQL
- Advanced Teradata SQL
- Physical Database Design
- Physical Database Tuning
- Teradata Application Utilities
- Teradata Parallel Transporter
- Teradata Warehouse Management
- Teradata Warehouse Administration
- Teradata Application Design and Development

NOTE: Formal education recommendations may vary based on previous training and relevant job experience.

Certification... Knowledge Building to Mastery

Competition is fierce. Differentiate yourself while building critical IT technology knowledge and skills. Trust Teradata Certification to help you build the expertise employers are looking for in a demanding, data-driven global business environment. Teradata developed a new generation of certification exams that bring premium value to Teradata 14 Certification credentials.

Top 10 "What's new about the Teradata 14 Certification Track?"

1. Seven exams with all new content based upon the following database releases: Teradata Database 13.0, Teradata Database 13.1, Teradata Database 14.0 (including SLES 11)
2. The *"Teradata 14 Bridge from Teradata 12"* Exam allows Teradata 12 certified candidates to move, or "bridge", from the Teradata 12 Certification track to the Teradata 14 Certification track without starting the track from the beginning.
3. Eligibility-based exams to ensure compliance with Teradata Certification requirements (Bridge and Masters exams only)
4. Teradata 12 Certified Masters will take just one exam to update to Teradata 14 Certified Master status.
5. A Qualification exam is not required for those that have achieved a Teradata 12 Master Certification.
6. A new Candidate Agreement and revised security measures are in place to protect the value of your investment and integrity of all exams and certifications.
7. Newly designed electronic certificates, wallet cards, and logos.
8. An easy Certification verification process for individuals and employers.
9. More rigorous certification criteria including a combination of training, study, and practical, hands-on experience.

10. A team of dedicated, experienced, and knowledgeable individuals with a passion to help you achieve your Teradata Certification goals!

Path to Teradata 14 Mastery

A Teradata Certified Master enjoys a distinct advantage in the global marketplace. Employers seek Teradata Certified staff with verifiable knowledge and skills that support their business-critical Teradata systems. The TCPP process helps those individuals who want to deepen their knowledge and build their skills to the highest level.

The path to achieve Teradata 14 Certified Master status is summarized in the matrix below.

If You Are...	Exams Required for Teradata 14 Master Certification
Starting on the Teradata 14 Certification Track	• TE0-141 – TE0-147 All 7 Exams required
Teradata 12 Certified Master	TE0-147: Teradata 14 Comprehensive Mastery Exam

Exam Registration

All Teradata Certification exams are administered and proctored by authorized Prometric Testing Centers. Schedule exams at any authorized Prometric Testing Center by phone or online. In the US and Canada, you may call 1-877-887-6868. A listing of Prometric telephone numbers, by country, is available at:

www.prometric.com/Teradata. Some countries do not offer online registration.

Where to Find More Information

Teradata Corporation's official certification exams and credentials are developed, copyrighted, and managed solely by the Teradata Certified Professional Program (TCPP) team. There are no other Teradata authorized exams, certifications, or legitimate credentials in the IT industry. To achieve your training and certification goals, pursue only authorized processes and approved courses of study as outlined on the official TCPP Website: www.Teradata.com/Certification. A mobile app with access to all study guides, practice questions, and many more Teradata Certification and related resources is also available for a variety of devices. Please refer to the web site for additional information.

Chapter 1: Teradata Product Overview

Certification Objectives

- ✓ Describe the features and benefits of the Teradata technology.
- ✓ Describe the basic concepts of Teradata Active Solutions: Active Load, Active Access, Active Workload Management, Active Events, Active Enterprise Integration, and Active Availability.

Before You Begin

You should be familiar with the following terms and concepts.

Terms	Key Concepts
Shared Nothing	Virtual processors dedicated to disks
Linear Scalability	Processing in parallel and data growth
Teradata Platforms	Hardware systems supported

The Teradata RDBMS

Teradata is a Relational Database Management System (RDBMS), manufactured by Teradata Corporation, and is designed to support databases ranging from less than one terabyte to thousands of terabytes. This makes Teradata an obvious choice for both mid-range and very large data warehousing applications. Teradata enables its customers to answer virtually any question about its business, and to provide them with the answers they need to compete in today's marketplace.

With its parallelism and scalability, Teradata allows you to start small and grow very large, through linear scalability. Teradata is an open system; it is compliant with industry ANSI standards. Teradata can be accessed using SQL (Structured Query Language), which is used as the basis for ad hoc requests, as well as Business Intelligence (BI) tool integration.

Unlike traditional Online Transaction Processing (OLTP) databases, which are designed for the rapid processing of small amounts of transactional data, Teradata is designed to be a data warehouse system. Data warehouse systems are designed to process large amounts of data, very quickly and efficiently.

Teradata's Unique Features

Single Data Store

Teradata's ability to store large amounts of data gives it the ability to store all of the organization's data, in a single repository. Unlike other RDBMS systems, where data is often fragmented and replicated across multiple data stores, the Teradata Database is built to accommodate the data for the entire enterprise.

Having a single data store eliminates the space overhead associated with multiple data stores, along with guaranteeing a single, centralized copy of the data. The potential for data discrepancies is minimized and database administrators are not burdened with the movement of data across disparate sources.

Multiple applications can concurrently connect to Teradata and query the database. With all the data in a single data store, an application can communicate with virtually all facets of the business.

Shared Nothing Architecture

Teradata is a Shared Nothing Architecture. Each Teradata node, and their AMPs, operates independently from the rest of the nodes. An

AMP, which is discussed further in Chapter 4, is referred to as an Access Module Processor (AMP). An AMP is responsible for data access. The AMPs each have their own disk space, which is not shared amongst the other AMPs, nor do AMPs connect directly to other AMPs.

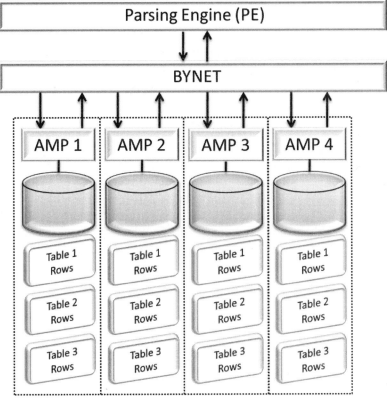

Figure 1.1

As illustrated in Figure 1.1, each AMP should have a relatively equal amount of rows from each table. Each AMP has a direct connection to the network via the BYNET. AMPs do not rely on each other to complete their individual assignments nor do they inhibit each other's operations.

Parallelism

The Teradata Database's high performance is directly attributable to its parallel design, and is referred to as having "unconditional parallelism". No special data models, column range constraints, or data quantities are required to make Teradata parallel; it is parallel by design. The Teradata Database is comprised of many separate virtual processors, all working in tandem, to answer a user's question.

Unlike OLTP systems, which are typically Symmetric Multi-Processing (SMP) based, Teradata is a Massively Parallel Processing (MPP) system. An MPP system outperforms SMP systems when processing large amounts of data, because an MPP system divides its workload evenly across its entire system, whereas an SMP system does not. Just as dividing up assignments across multiple employees allows more work to get accomplished in a short amount of time, Teradata splits up its assignments amongst its worker processes, allowing for more queries and larger amounts of data to be processed in a shorter period of time.

Linear Scalability

Linear scalability ensures that Teradata is highly scalable (currently up to 1024 nodes). Linear scalability dictates that performance will improve, and not diminish, as the system grows. The addition of AMPs will proportionately increase a system's performance capabilities. Basically, you can double the performance of a Teradata system by doubling the number of AMPs and their supporting nodes. Figure 1.2 depicts the doubling of AMPs on our sample Teradata system.

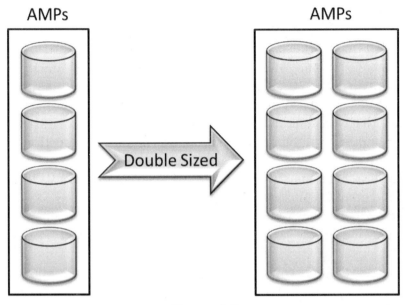

Figure 1.2

Scalability translates into flexibility and affordability. A scalable system means that it can start small and grow according to the needs of the business, without the threat of system degradation, as the system grows in size.

Mature Optimizer

The Teradata Database Optimizer (discussed in further detail -- Chapter 4) has been refined and enhanced throughout Teradata's history. While the basic concepts of the Teradata Database have changed little since its inception, Teradata has continued to innovate and re-architect its Optimizer. With each new version of the Teradata RDBMS, the Optimizer has become more mature and robust.

Unlike other data warehouse platforms, the Teradata Database Optimizer has the ability to perform multiple complex queries, multiple joins within a query, and virtually unlimited ad hoc processing. In addition, because the Optimizer is built in accordance with the Teradata Database's parallelism, it develops least-cost query plans that are both efficient and parallel.

Automatic Data Distribution

The Teradata Database automatically manages the distribution of data on its database. Other data warehouse platforms require manual intervention by the DBAs to efficiently distribute the data, in order to improve performance. Teradata handles the distribution, without requiring manual effort or distribution strategies.

Teradata Active Solutions

In an active data warehouse, Teradata provides both strategic intelligence and operational intelligence.

- Strategic intelligence entails delivering intelligence through tools and utilities and query mechanisms that support strategic decision-making.

  This includes, for example, providing users with simple as well as complex reports throughout the day which indicate the business trends that have occurred and that are occurring, which show why such trends occurred, and which predict if they will continue to occur.

- Operational intelligence entails delivering intelligence through tools and utilities and query mechanisms that support front-line or operational decision-making. This includes, for example, ensuring aggressive Service Level Goals (SLGs) with respect to high performance, data freshness, and system availability.

Active Access

Teradata is able to access analytical intelligence quickly and consistently in support of operational business processes.

But the benefit of Active Access entails more than just speeding up user and customer requests. Active Access provides intelligence for operational and customer interactions consistently.

Active Access queries; also referred to as tactical queries, support tactical decision-making at the front-line. Such queries can be informational, such as simply retrieving a customer record or transaction, or they may include complex analytics.

Active Availability

Teradata is able to meet business objectives for its own availability. Moreover, it assists customers in identifying application-specific availability, recoverability, and performance requirements based on the impact of enterprise downtime. Teradata can also recommend strategies for achieving system availability goals.

Active Enterprise Integration

Teradata is able to integrate itself into enterprise business and technical architectures, especially those that support business users, partners, and customers. This simplifies the task of coordinating enterprise applications and business processes.

For example, a Teradata event, generated from a database trigger, calls a stored procedure, which inserts a row into a queue table and publishes a message via the Teradata JMS Provider. The message is delivered to a JMS queue on a WebLogic, SAP NetWeaver, or other JMScompatible application server. SAP Customer Relationship

Management receives the message, notifies the user, and takes an action.

Active Events

Teradata is able to detect a business event automatically, apply business rules against current and historical data, and initiate operational actions when appropriate. This enables enterprises to reduce the latency between the identification of an event and taking action with respect to it. Active Events entails more than event detection.

When notified of something important, Teradata presents users with recommendations for appropriate action. The analysis done for users may prescribe the best course of action or give them alternatives from which to choose.

Active Load

Teradata is able to load data actively and in a non-disruptive manner and, at the same time, process other workloads.

Teradata delivers Active Load through methods that support continuous data loading. These include streaming from a queue, more frequent batch updates, and moving changed data from another database platform to Teradata.

These methods exercise such Teradata Database features as queue tables and triggers, and use FastLoad, MultiLoad, TPump, standalone utilities, and Teradata Parallel Transporter.

Teradata can effectively manage a complex workload environment on a "single version of the business."

Active Workload Management

Teradata is able to manage mixed workloads dynamically and to optimize system resource utilization to meet business goals.

Teradata Active System Management (ASM) is a portfolio of products that enables real-time system management.

Teradata ASM assists the database administrator in analyzing and establishing workloads and resource allocation to meet business needs. Teradata ASM facilitates monitoring workload requests to ensure that resources are used efficiently and that dynamic workloads are prioritized automatically.

Teradata ASM also provides state-of-the-art techniques to visualize the current operational environment and to analyze long-term trends. Teradata ASM enables database administrators to set SLGs, to monitor adherence to them, and to take any necessary steps to reallocate resources to meet business objectives.

Supported Platforms

Operating Systems

All of the Teradata Database Systems now use Novell SUSE Linux (64-bit) as their operating system.

The Purpose-Built Family Platform

Teradata offers a variety of platforms that are designed to meet specific analytical needs. Each platform utilizes the Teradata Database, giving customers a heterogeneous platform that allows for the reuse of data models, ETL, and underlying structures. Whether it is an active data warehouse, enterprise data warehouse, entry-level data warehouse, special purpose data mart, or a test and development environment, there is a platform that supports each business requirement.

Teradata Extreme Data Appliance 1550

The Teradata Extreme Data Appliance 1550 is designed for the processing of massive data volume and for strategic analytics. It is highly scalable, and is based on the processing design of the Teradata Active Data Warehouse 5550 platform. This platform is intended for a smaller number of users, who are typically working outside of the Enterprise Data Warehouse (EDW), to accomplish a specific business objective.

Teradata Data Mart Appliance 2500/2550/2555

The Teradata Data Mart Appliance 2500/2550/2555 is designed for very fast data access and deep-dive analytics. This platform is pre-configured and ready to run, allowing customers to rapidly implement the appliance into their environment. The Teradata Data Mart Appliance includes a powerful set of Teradata's Tools and Utilities, which enable customers to easily migrate to the EDW.

Teradata Integrated Data Warehouse 5500H and 5555 C/H

The Teradata Active Enterprise Data Warehouse platform is designed for active data warehousing. This platform is designed and optimized for strategic and operational mixed workloads, high performance, power, and scalability. This platform is designed for full-scale EDW implementations and provides for the highest concurrency of users and applications.

Chapter 1: Practice Questions

1. Which feature is not unique to Teradata?
   A. Linear Scalability
   B. ANSI SQL
   C. Parallelism
   D. Single Data Store

2. Which of the following describes Linear Scalability?
   A. Double the number of PEs and performance doubles
   B. Double the number of AMPs and performance triples
   C. Double the number of disk drives and performance doubles
   D. Double the number of AMPs and their supporting nodes and performance doubles

3. In the phrase "aggressive SLG", what does SLG stand for?
   A. Service Local Goal
   B. Service Level Goal
   C. State and Local Government
   D. Super Light Gun
   E. Service Level Ghoul

4. Which Active Solution includes FastLoad, MultiLoad, TPump, and TPT?
   A. Active Access
   B. Active Availability
   C. Active Enterprise Integration
   D. Active Events
   E. Active Load
   F. Active Workload Management

5. Which Active Solution includes taking steps to reallocate resources to meet business needs?
    A. Active Access
    B. Active Availability
    C. Active Enterprise Integration
    D. Active Events
    E. Active Load
    F. Active Workload Management

6. Which Active Solution enables enterprises to reduce the latency between the identification of an event and taking action with respect to it?
    A. Active Access
    B. Active Availability
    C. Active Enterprise Integration
    D. Active Events
    E. Active Load
    F. Active Workload Management

7. Which Active Solution allows Teradata to interface with different architectures?
    A. Active Access
    B. Active Availability
    C. Active Enterprise Integration
    D. Active Events
    E. Active Load
    F. Active Workload Management

Chapter Notes

Utilize this space for notes, key points to remember, diagrams, areas of further study, etc.

Chapter 2: Data Warehouse Architectures

Certification Objectives

- ✓ Describe the layers of the Enterprise data warehouse architecture.
- ✓ Identify the components of a data warehouse architecture.
- ✓ Contrast centrally located architectures with physically distributed architectures, such as an appliance.
- ✓ Determine the benefits of centralized data warehouses vs. non-centralized data warehouses.
- ✓ Describe the approach of building an application data model vs. Enterprise data model.
- ✓ Describe the characteristics of row vs. set processing.

Before You Begin

You should be familiar with the following terms and concepts.

Terms	Key Concepts
Data Layers	Staging, physical, and semantic layers
Active Data Warehousing	Evolution of data warehousing
Data Processing Options	OLTP, DSS, OLAP, and Data Mining
Data Processing Types	Row and Set Processing

Data Layers

The data in an EDW is managed, manipulated, and queried, in a variety of ways. Depending on the intended function, the method of handling data will vary. The data warehouse is considered to have three distinct data layers, which are classified by the mechanisms used to access and process the data as illustrated in Figure 2.1.

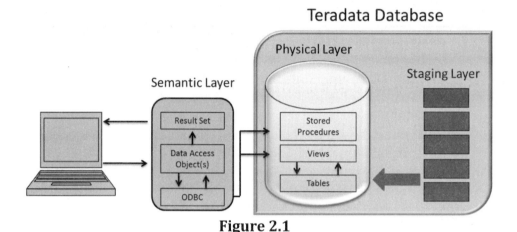

Figure 2.1

Staging Layer

The staging layer is the data extraction, load, and transformation area. Whether an ETL or ELT process is utilized, this is the layer where data is physically inserted into the data warehouse, in preparation for its full integration into the main tables in the database.

Physical Layer

The physical layer is where the data is structured for flexible, efficient, and business-friendly access. Denormalizations such as summary tables and pre-aggregations are built to provide the user with query flexibility and efficiency. In addition, Join Indexes (discussed in further detail - Chapter 5) are also utilized to improve query performance.

Access Layer

The access layer, which is often call the semantic layer, is the business representation of the data. It is defined using business terms and is considered to be the access layer. Business Intelligence (BI) tools, cubes, and views are used to access this layer.

Active Data Warehousing

Evolution

As a data warehouse grows, and as it is further integrated into the day-to-day operations of the business, the ways in which the data warehouse is used begins to change. At first, data warehouses often solve a reporting need. Once fully implemented, the data warehouse can be used to achieve Active Enterprise Intelligence. Data warehouse usage typically evolves through five different stages beginning with Reporting, to Analyzing, to Predicting, to Operationalizing, and finally, to Active Data Warehousing.

Stages of Data Warehouse Evolution

Stage 1 – Reporting

Initially, data warehouses are most often used for historical reporting, such as monthly/quarterly/annual reporting. Reports are pre-defined, and used to provide basic information and analysis.

Stage 2 – Analyzing

Once reporting is established, attention turns towards analyzing the results. At this stage, one tries to determine why the actions occurred as well as begin to discover patterns in the data. Ad hoc queries and detail data analysis become more prevalent as you decipher additional meaning from the data.

Stage 3 – Predicting

After thorough analysis of the data, and once you have insight into what has occurred, the data warehouse is then used to predict what will happen in the future. Data mining tools and predictive models use historical data to forecast future results.

Stage 4 – Operationalizing

The data warehouse is moving from a strategic decision engine, into a tactical decisioning operation. Knowledge from the prior stages, which is typically available only to those working in a strategic role in the organization, becomes readily available to people in the organization that are making day-to-day decisions.

Stage 5 – Active Data Warehousing

Once the data warehouse is operationalized, it migrates toward full automation and becomes deeply integrated into most aspects of the enterprise's real-time operations. This stage is known as Active Data Warehousing. The data warehouse becomes involved in real time decisioning, such as displaying personalized offers to a customer on a web site, or performing complex customer operations, such as booking an airline reservation.

Active Enterprise Intelligence

Active Enterprise Intelligence (AEI) is achieved once the Active Data Warehouse is fully integrated into the customer's business and technical architecture, providing 24/7 availability. As a result, the Teradata Database is sufficiently able to handle large volumes of data, mixed workloads (strategic and tactical), concurrent users and applications, and the responsiveness needed to provide virtually minute-to-minute information.

Breaking down each word in AEI, it is "active" in that it has the capability to drive intelligent decisioning, efficiently and on-demand. It supports the "enterprise" by providing a single view of the whole business, to both users and applications across the business. Finally, the "intelligence" is derived from its ability to support both tactical and strategic decisioning, by aligning all of the enterprise's systems and business processes. The Teradata Active Data Warehouse (ADW) is all of Teradata's products, services, features, and business partnerships, combined together, in order to support the Active Enterprise Intelligence business strategy.

Evolution of Data Processing

In the past, data processing was separated into two distinct segments, Online Transaction Processing (OLTP) and Decision Support Systems (DSS). Today, data processing can be broken into four distinct segments, OLTP, DSS, OLAP, and Data Mining.

Online Transaction Processing (OLTP)

Online Transaction Processing systems are designed to support a large volume and high frequency of user requests in real time. However, these requests typically require a small set of rows and limited data processing. Typically, OLTP systems are purely transactional systems, such as web sites and ATMs.

Decision Support Systems (DSS)

Decision Support Systems are designed to process much larger data volumes than OLTP systems, and to perform data analysis, as opposed to real time transactions. DSS receives fewer requests than OLTP, but the requests are typically much more complex, and involve many rows and tables. A DSS is used to analyze detail data to look for historical trends, detect patterns, and make future predictions.

Online Analytical Processing (OLAP)

OLAP is a type of analytical processing found within a Decision Support System. OLAP data cubes allow for the "slicing and dicing" of facts along dimensions. This provides the user with greater insight into the data, greater flexibility in the amount of questions that can be asked and even quicker answers to complex business questions. A variety of generic OLAP tools are available, which facilitate the creation of the cubes and the reporting of the results.

Data Mining

In Data Mining, deep analysis of historical data is performed in order to discover patterns. These patterns are then used to create predictive models, which are used to determine future actions. Data Mining is very useful for forecasting purposes, such as customer purchase and inventory forecasting, churn analysis, and fraud detection.

Data Mining has two distinct phases. In the first phase, an analytic model is built, based on historical detail data. In the second phase, the model is applied to current data, in order to predict what may occur in the future (based on the past events found in the historical data).

Distributed Architecture

A true Enterprise Data Warehouse is a single platform with a centralized architecture, with all hardware and software components fully integrated. However, a physically distributed architecture describes a system where the data warehouse itself is distributed across multiple hardware and software components.

Depending on its usage, a data warehouse might fit either architecture. For example, a data warehouse that contains all of the enterprise data would be considered a centralized architecture. If a data warehouse only contains a portion of the enterprise data for a specific application purpose (i.e., Customer Relationship Management), it would be considered physically distributed in that it is separate from the EDW.

Centralized Data Warehouse

The purpose of a data warehouse is to act as a single centralized data store for the entire enterprise. Data from all operational systems are extracted and loaded into the data warehouse to provide a holistic view of the entire organization.

The centralized data warehouse eliminates the need for multiple, non-centralized data warehouses. Having a single, centralized data warehouse allows for cross-business analysis against accurate and timely data. Non-centralized data warehouses often contain inconsistent data and offer limited answers to complex business questions.

Figure 2.2 illustrates a non-centralized data warehouse. In this scenario, an end-user must query each source system, individually. Because each system is isolated from one another, cross-business questions are difficult to answer. For example, imagine a question such as "do customers call more often when the inventory is depleted for a popular product". This question is not easy to answer because the data resides in separate locations and cannot be queried on the same system.

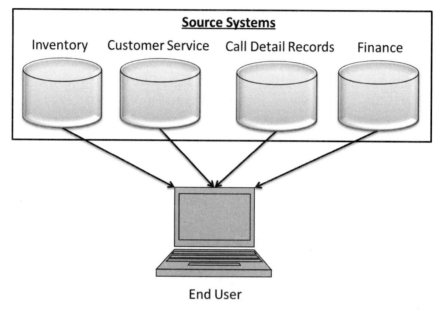

Figure 2.2

Figure 2.3 illustrates the centralized data warehouse. The end-user is able to query the Teradata Data Warehouse as a single data source as opposed to each individual system. In addition, the end-user has the ability to join the data from different source systems together in their queries to answer cross-business questions.

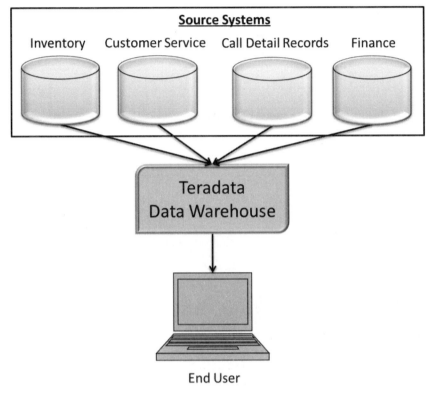

Figure 2.3

Data Marts

A data mart is a subset of data that is used to support a specific function or application. A data mart may contain both detail and summary data, but this data is often structured specifically (aggregated or filtered) for its intended application. There are three types of data marts: Independent, Logical, and Dependent. Figure 2.4 depicts how the different types of data marts might interact with a Teradata system.

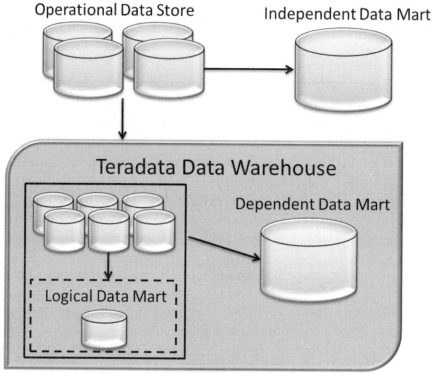

Figure 2.4

Independent Data Marts

Independent data marts are subsets of data that are sourced from one or more operational systems. The data is in a separate physical location from the originating data. In some cases, independent data marts can contain detail for a specific subject, but it is typically summarized and aggregated, and used for specific business applications.

Although independent data marts are easy to build, and may support smaller business requirements, they are costly to support. Data must be moved between sources, additional storage costs are required, and the data must be synchronized consistently and accurately. In addition, because the detail data usually does not exist on the independent data mart, only a limited number of questions can be asked of the data.

Logical Data Marts

Logical data marts are located in the same physical location as the rest of the data warehouse. Because an EDW stores all of the data for the business, it is relatively easy to create a virtual, or logical, data mart within the same data warehouse system. In Teradata, this is accomplished by a view layer, and enables the data mart to access all detail data from the rest of the data warehouse and minimizes data extraction, loads, and transformations.

A drawback to logical data marts is that they rely on the use of the detail data in the data warehouse, which is not aggregated or dimensionalized. However, Teradata's parallelism, and its ability to act as a single data store enables logical data marts to co-exist with the rest of the data warehouse, without significantly impacting performance.

Dependent Data Marts

A dependent data mart is a subset of data that is created directly from the detail data in the data warehouse. Like an independent data mart, it requires the loading and transformation of data, and creates a separate repository of data. However, like the logical data mart the data may also reside on the EDW as well as a separate platform (i.e., a Teradata Appliance). Dependent data marts provide more flexibility than independent data marts, and have all of the advantages of the logical data mart.

Processing Types and Characteristics

Enterprise and Application Data Models

An Enterprise Data Model is used to map the entire enterprise. All aspects of the business, rather than a specific group, are included, in order to represent the entire organization. An Application Data Model is specific to a particular application, functional group, or area of the business.

In an Enterprise Data Warehouse, an Enterprise Data Model should be leveraged, as opposed to an Application Data Model, because the Enterprise Data Model encompasses all aspects of the business. An Enterprise Data Model provides the data warehouse with the flexibility to answer all questions across the organization, without regard to any specific business application.

Row and Set Processing

Depending on its design, a database can utilize one of two methods to process rows of data: row-by-row or set processing. Regardless of the chosen method, the rows are updated with a single command. However, each method has its distinctive qualities.

Row-by-Row Processing

In row-by-row processing, a single row is retrieved, and then the processing operation is performed, such as an update, insert, or delete. After that row has been processed, each subsequent row is completed and processed (one at-a-time) until all rows have been processed. Row-by-row does have an advantage over set processing, in that only one row is locked at-a-time, causing less lock contention (more than one user trying to access the same row, simultaneously) to occur.

Set Processing

In set processing, a set of relational data rows can be processed at once, without the need to process one at-a-time. This is significantly faster than row-by-row, in that 10 to 30 times the amount of data can be updated, at once. Set processing takes advantage of parallelism, and distributes the processing across all of the AMPs, in order to complete the data operation. Set processing is much more advantageous than row-by-row processing, when updating large volumes of data.

Chapter 2: Practice Questions

1. Which layer is used for ETL/ELT processing?
   A. Staging
   B. Physical
   C. Semantic
   D. Access

2. What does the acronym AEI stand for?
   A. Associated Evolution Intelligence
   B. Active Enterprise Involvement
   C. Abstract Information
   D. Active Enterprise Intelligence

3. Which segment of data processing involves deep dives into historical data to build predictive   models?
   A. DSS
   B. OLTP
   C. OLAP
   D. Data mining

4. Which segment of data processing involves a few rows and limited processing?
   A. DSS
   B. OLTP
   C. OLAP
   D. Data mining

5. Which of the following is not a data mart?
   A. Dependent Data Mart
   B. Independent Data Mart
   C. Integrated Data Mart
   D. Logical Data Mart

6. Which data mart relies on detail data that has not been aggregated or dimensionalized?
   A. Dependent Data Mart
   B. Independent Data Mart
   C. Integrated Data Mart
   D. Logical Data Mart

Chapter Notes

Utilize this space for notes, key points to remember, diagrams, areas of further study, etc.

Chapter 3: Relational Database Concepts

Certification Objectives

- ✓ Define the terms associated with relational concepts.
- ✓ Describe the advantages of a relational database.
- ✓ Describe the differences between star schema and third normal form logical models.

Before You Begin

You should be familiar with the following terms and concepts.

Terms	Key Concepts
Logical Data Modeling	Primary and Foreign Keys,
Normalization	Types and descriptions of forms
Dimensional Modeling	Fact / Dimension, and Star Schema

Logical Data Modeling

A Logical Data Model (LDM) is a logical representation of the entities (and their attributes), and their inter-relationships within a company's organization. The LDM helps to provide an illustrated version of the business requirements.

The LDM describes the data structure of each entity, along with sample data. The depicted entities model real world entities such as people, places and things. The LDM is designed irrespective of its usage or data volumes.

Primary key and foreign key attributes are designated to provide an understanding of the entity's unique identifier and its relationships. Establishing relationships helps to illustrate the "big picture" of the model by showing how the entities inter-relate.

Figure 3.1 demonstrates a small portion of an LDM:

Entity: EMPLOYEE

Column Name:	EMP	DEPT	LNAME	FNAME	SALARY
Notations:	PK	FK			
Sample Data:	258	99	Lawson	Judy	205000
	369	01	Gatsby	Walter	100000
	654	25	Valdez	Jorge	30000

Figure 3.1

Primary Keys

A primary key is the designated attribute (or attributes) in an entity whose unique values will be used to identify each row in the entity. Most often, the best candidate is one small attribute that most appropriately represents the data in the row. Occasionally, multiple attributes may be necessary to serve as a primary key, in order to guarantee uniqueness.

Figure 3.2 shows the Customer and Area entities. The Customer entity has CUST_ID as its primary key, and the Area entity has AREA as its primary key.

Entity: CUSTOMER

CUST_ID (PK)	AREA (FK)	LAST_NM	FIRST_NM
333	3	Roark	Oscar
369	4	Gatsby	Walter
665	2	Mendoza	Manny

Entity: AREA

AREA (PK)	AREA_NAME
1	North
2	South
3	East
4	West

Figure 3.2

Foreign Keys

A foreign key is one or more attributes in an entity that relates to a primary key in another entity. A foreign key cannot have a non-null value without a corresponding value in the primary key entity.

Primary Key Compared to Foreign Key

Although Primary and Foreign Keys are used in conjunction to relate data together, there are some key differences between the two:

Primary Key
- Must not be null
- No duplicate values allowed
- Only one primary key per entity

Foreign Key
- Foreign key must have a corresponding primary key
- An entity can have zero or more foreign keys
- Duplicate values are allowed
- Null values are allowed

Figure 3.3 shows the same Customer and Area entities as in the previous example. Notice that the AREA attribute also appears in the Customer entity and it is designated as a foreign key. The attribute points back to the AREA attribute in the Area entity, where it is the primary key.

Entity: CUSTOMER

CUST_ID (PK)	AREA (FK)	LAST_NM	FIRST_NM
333	3	Roark	Oscar
369	4	Gatsby	Walter
665	2	Mendoza	Manny

Entity: AREA

AREA (PK)	AREA_NAME
1	North
2	South
3	East
4	West

Figure 3.3

Normalization

Normalization describes a series of techniques that are used to design database tables. These techniques, incorporated into the data model, help reduce redundancy and avoid structural problems that lead to data anomalies. Normalization ensures that the database design is well-formed and that it is not redundant. A normalized model includes entities, attributes, and relationships.

Normalization is broken down into different degrees referred to as "forms". Each form of normalization encompasses the form(s) before it. Below is a brief description of the first three normal forms.

First Normal Form (1NF)

1NF ensures the table/entity is free of repeating groups. For example, the employee table would not contain phone numbers, because every employee probably has more than one number, which would lead to repeating groups of data (i.e. phone numbers).

Second Normal Form (2NF)

2NF ensures that all columns/attributes must relate to the entire primary key and not just part of the key. For example, the employee table does not need a combination of employee id and last name. Only employee id is relevant in the relation.

Third Normal Form (3NF)

3NF ensures that all columns relate only to the primary key, and not to any other column. For example, the employee sales table should only contain sales information, and not irrelevant information, such as employee birth date, which belongs in the employee table.

A good data warehouse is in 3NF, because it helps to avoid redundant data, saves disk space, and reduces unsynchronized data. Eliminating redundant data strengthens data integrity and requires fewer updates to keep the EDW data in sync.

Dimensional Modeling

Fact Tables

Fact tables contain numeric measurements (such as aggregates, averages, and summations) or other fact information. Examples are sales totals, unit totals, quantities, etc. Fact tables primarily store the most important and quantifiable data about a business process. The fact table is surrounded by dimension tables, which are used to analyze or "dimension" the data within the fact table.

Table: FACT_SALES

DATE_ID	PRODUCT_ID	STORE_ID	SALES_TOTAL	QUANTITY
23	69354	201	97244.78	233
32	54897	954	95564.45	1510
43	44577	400	78724.49	855

Figure 3.4

In Figure 3.4, we have a table named FACT_SALES. This is a fact table that contains information about product sales, at a given store, on a given day. The primary key is comprised of a date id, a product id, and a store id. The FACT_SALES represents an intersection with the product, date, and store dimensions.

Dimension Tables

Dimension tables are used to describe the information in fact tables, and are composed of attributes that are used for grouping, constraining, and reporting fact table data. The data contains the properties and characteristics of the object (i.e., product). The data in dimension tables is deep and is useful for querying and reporting. Without dimension tables, the information in fact tables would have little business meaning to the end-user.

Table: DIM_PRODUCT

PRODUCT_ID	PRODUCT_NAME	PRODUCT_MANUF	PRODUCT_CATEGORY
69354	Handy Wrench	2341	11
54897	Big Drill	5644	11
44577	Power Screwdriver	3525	35

Figure 3.5

In Figure 3.5, we have a dimension table named "DIM_PRODUCT". This table contains information about individual products, such as the product id, the product name, the product manufacturer, and the product category. Queries against the DIM_PRODUCT table provide the user with detailed information about the actual product, versus a fact table, which would only indicate that a particular product had been sold.

Star Schema

The dimensional model, which is composed of the dimension and fact tables, is commonly referred to as a Star Schema (also known as the Star Join Schema). In a star schema model, a fact table is surrounded by its related dimension tables. The star schema model is designed to be flexible, and this allows for the addition of new facts and dimensions. Dimensions and facts can be modified without significant impact to the rest of the system. A Snowflake Schema is another type of star schema that is commonly used in dimensional modeling.

A benefit of star schema is easier querying, flexibility, and improved performance. Query performance improves because the tables are joined together directly, rather than through complicated, multi-table relationships. Because there are fewer columns in the fact tables, less information must be processed, resulting in better performance. Dimensions ensure that many different questions can be asked, using the same base information, without query optimizations having to be made for each question asked.

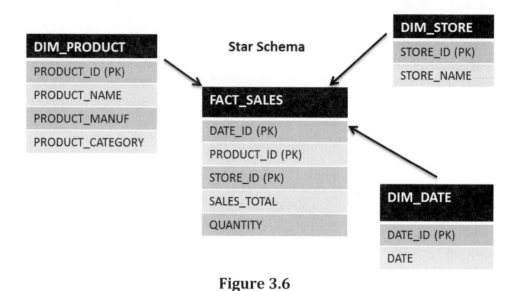

Figure 3.6

Figure 3.6 illustrates a sample star schema, made up of a single fact table, FACT_SALES, surrounded by product, store, and date dimension tables.

Star Schema vs. 3NF Model

The star schema, which is the most common form of denormalization used in contemporary data warehousing, cannot handle every kind of relationship that can exist comfortably in a fully normalized environment. Variable level recursive relationships are one such example.

Also, you cannot make the universal assumption that all levels in a dimensional model are balanced. A star schema dimension table, which requires fixed columns for each level, has considerable difficulty in handling unbalanced hierarchies.

A star schema is designed specifically to support dimensional analysis, but not all analysis is dimensional. Many types of quantitative analysis, such as data mining, statistical analysis, and case-based reasoning, are actually inhibited by a physical star schema design.

Formulating queries to address novel requirements is made more difficult, if not impossible, in a denormalized environment. A fully normalized enterprise data model is flexible enough to support the undertaking of any new analyses of the data.

More importantly, you can create "denormalized" views to implement a semantic layer that makes the normalized data model easier to navigate. Few sites permit users to query base tables directly anyway, so creating views on base tables that look exactly like their denormalized table counterparts should not be an issue.

By handling denormalization virtually, the relationships within, between, and among the underlying base tables of the schema remain intact, and referential integrity can be maintained by the system regardless of how many virtual denormalized relationships are created. This flexibility frees DBAs to create any number of denormalized views for users while simultaneously maintaining semantic data integrity and eliminating the data redundancies required by denormalized physical schemas.

DBAs can create virtual, subject-oriented schemas for specific applications as well as creating views for more general database access without affecting the underlying base table data. These same views can also be used to enforce security constraints for the different communities of business users who must access the database.

Chapter 3: Practice Questions

1. Which definition applies to foreign keys?
    A. Must be Not Null
    B. Only one per table
    C. Must not be changed
    D. May not contain duplicate values
    E. May be null

2. Which Normal Form eliminates repeating values in a table?
    A. First Normal Form (1NF)
    B. Second Normal Form (2NF)
    C. Third Normal Form (3NF)
    D. Fourth Normal Form (4NF)

3. Which Normal Form requires that non-key attributes relate to the entire Primary Key and not just a portion?
    A. First Normal Form (1NF)
    B. Second Normal Form (2NF)
    C. Third Normal Form (3NF)
    D. Fourth Normal Form (4NF)

4. Which Normal Form requires all columns to relate only to the Primary Key and not each other?
    A. First Normal Form (1NF)
    B. Second Normal Form (2NF)
    C. Third Normal Form (3NF)
    D. Fourth Normal Form (4NF)

5. Which definition does not apply to Primary Keys?
    A. May not contain nulls
    B. May not be changed
    C. May not contain duplicate values
    D. Must not contain more than one column

6. Which definition does not apply to Foreign Keys?
   A. A corresponding Primary Key is optional
   B. May contain null values
   C. Duplicate values are allowed
   D. Zero, one, or more are allowed per table

7. Which two statements are true? (choose two)
   A. Dimensional models are process oriented
   B. Relational models are process oriented
   C. Dimensional models are enterprise oriented
   D. Relational models are enterprise oriented
   E. Fact tables contain only detail data
   F. 3NF tables contain aggregated data

Chapter Notes

Utilize this space for notes, key points to remember, diagrams, areas of further study, etc.

Chapter 4: Teradata RDBMS Components and Architecture

Certification Objectives

- ✓ Describe the functionality of components of the Teradata technology.
- ✓ Identify the communication interfaces from external applications to Teradata.
- ✓ Identify application programming interfaces.
- ✓ Define perm space, spool space, and temp space.
- ✓ Identify the benefits of Teradata automatically managed storage vs. Database Administrator (DBA) manually managed distribution techniques

Before You Begin

You should be familiar with the following terms and concepts.

Terms	Key Concepts
PE	Parses, optimizes, and dispatches queries
BYNET	Communication layer
AMP	Accesses and manages the data
Database Space	Perm, Spool, and Temp
Connectivity	ODBC, JDBC, and CLI

Parsing Engine (PE)

The Parsing Engine's (PE) purpose is to formulate the most efficient and least expensive plan in order to return the requested response set. The Parsing Engine consists of the Parser, the Optimizer, and the Dispatcher. The plan is converted to executable steps, which are performed by the AMPs, and finally passed to the Dispatcher. The PE is also responsible for any necessary input conversions, such as a character set conversion from EBCDIC to ASCII.

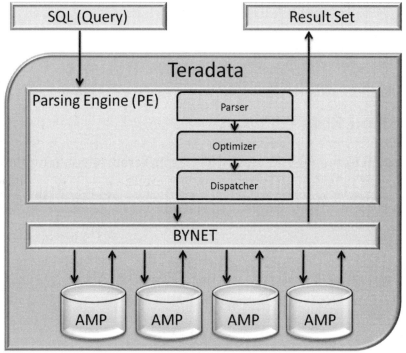

Figure 4.1

As illustrated in Figure 4.1, for every submitted request, the PE:

1. Manipulates session-control activities (e.g., logon, authentication, logoff, and restores sessions after client or server failures.
2. Verifies the syntax of the request (SQL)
3. Verifies the user's security permissions to determine if the target object (table, views, macros, etc.) can be accessed
4. Parses and optimizes SQL
5. Formulates the execution plan for the AMPs which includes breaking down the actual request into a series of steps
6. Returns result answer set back to the client

Teradata BYNET

The Parsing Engine does not communicate directly to the AMPs. Instead, a communication layer, known as the BYNET, sits between the AMPs and PEs. The PE transmits the plan to the AMPs via the BYNET. In response, the data that the AMPs retrieve from disk drives is returned to the PE via the BYNET. Each Teradata configuration has two BYNET channels (providing redundancy and additional bandwidth). The channels are bi-directional pathways that send and receive data concurrently, as illustrated in Figure 4.2.

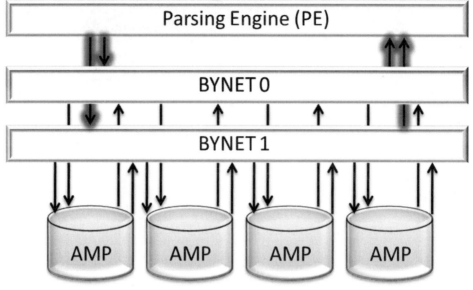

Figure 4.2

Access Module Processors (AMPs)

The Access Module Processors (AMPs) perform the physical task of retrieving the result data. AMPs also perform any necessary output conversions, such as data type conversions. The AMPs connect to a single virtual disk (VDISK), which is discussed further in Chapter 6.

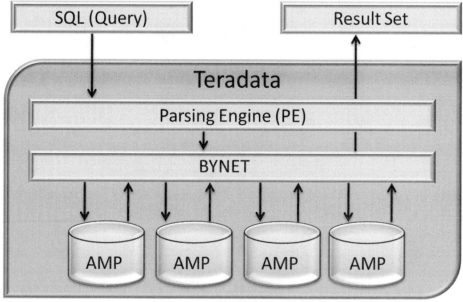

Figure 4.3

Figure 4.3 reveals how the AMPs operate. The rows of each table on a Teradata system are distributed evenly across all the AMPs and each AMP is responsible for the row retrieval for each table on their disk. The AMPs work independently and therefore retrieve data concurrently. Each AMP performs its portion of the work in parallel, which is a foundation of parallel processing. The AMPs are also responsible for aggregating columns, lock management, sorting rows, join processing, output formatting, disk space management, accounting, recovery processing, and special utility protocols.

Nodes

Teradata refers to each individual server within a system as a node, which is comprised of both hardware and software. Each node has its own operating system (OS), its own copy of the Teradata RDMBS software, CPUs, memory, and disk space.

In turn, a Teradata cabinet is comprised of one or more nodes, and a system can have more than one cabinet. Each node is connected to the BYNET, which is the communication path for the entire system.

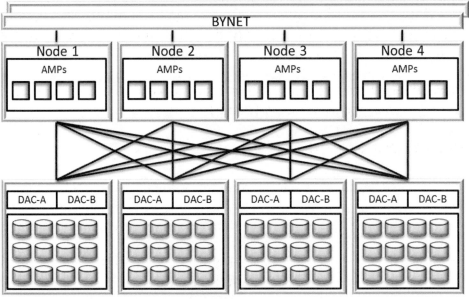

Figure 4.4

In Figure 4.4, we have a four node Teradata system. Each node has two Intel® processors and up to 32 GB of memory where the AMPs and PEs are configured. This is why AMPs and PEs are referred to as Virtual Processors (VPROCs). The node connects to both the BYNET and to a disk array, which is a set of disks. The disk array is where the AMP's share of table data is physically stored.

Space Allocation

In Teradata, space allocation is defined as the amount of disk space that is permitted for a specific user or database. Space allocation acts as a ceiling, or upper-limit, not as a guaranteed amount. The amount of space a user or database can physically consume is based upon the actual space availability on the Teradata system.

Teradata has three different categories of space allocation: Permanent (Perm), Spool, and Temporary (Temp).

Permanent (Perm) Space

Permanent (Perm) space is the amount of data storage allowed for a specific user or database. This data storage includes the actual table data, secondary index sub-tables, fallback table data, and permanent journals. Perm space allocation is not a guarantee. If there is no more usable space available on any AMP for a specific user or database, a user or database cannot utilize its full definition.

With a new installation of Teradata, all Perm space in Teradata is owned by the system master account, DBC. The total amount of Perm space on the Teradata system would be the sum of all available Perm space, across all AMPs, divided by the number of AMPs. Available Perm space is always determined per AMP because Teradata distributes data as evenly as possible across all AMPs.

In Figure 4.5, we have a new Teradata system with 10 AMPs and 1 terabyte of total system disk space, which is currently owned by DBC. Divided by AMP, we have 100 GB of actual available disk space which defines the per AMP limit.

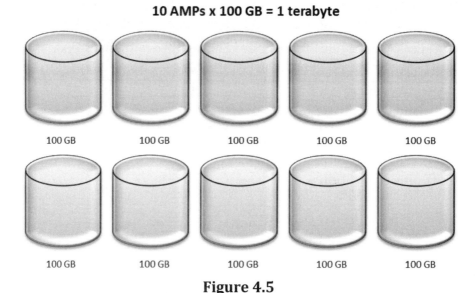

10 AMPs x 100 GB = 1 terabyte

100 GB   100 GB   100 GB   100 GB   100 GB

100 GB   100 GB   100 GB   100 GB   100 GB

Figure 4.5

Perm Space Limits and Hierarchy

User accounts and databases exist in Teradata as part of a hierarchical structure. The DBC user is the master, and sits on top of the entire Teradata hierarchy. When a new user or database is added to the system, a parent user must be designated. Once created, a user can have its own child users and/or databases, which can, in turn, have their own child users and/or databases.

In Teradata, space allocation is driven by the hierarchy. When a new database (or user) is created, it will need to have space available for the creation of tables and other objects. The amount of allocated space is zero at creation; there is no default value that may be specified. The parent database (or user) must give the new database some of its own allocated space. However, the amount of space allocated to a child database or user can be zero.

Once space is allocated to the new database, the space available to the parent is deducted and given to the child. However, if the child database is dropped, the space allocation is automatically returned to the parent. Likewise, when table data is deleted, or when a table (or other object) is dropped, the space is returned to the parent database/user.

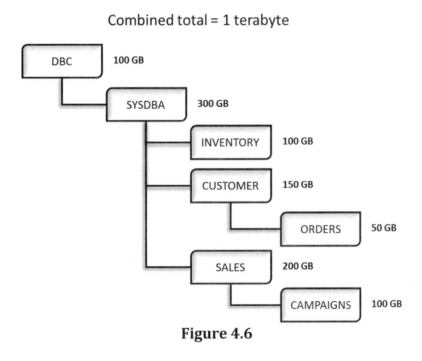

Figure 4.6

Figure 4.6 illustrates a 1 terabyte Teradata system in which DBC has dispensed 600 GB of its Perm space to the Sales, Inventory, and Customer databases. The Sales database, which originally had 300 GB of allocated space, has given 100 GB of space to its child database, Campaigns. The Customer database has given 50 GB of its space to Orders. If the Campaigns or Orders database is dropped, their space will be return to their respective parent.

Spool Space

Spool space is the disk space that is used to store a submitted query's intermediate and final result sets. All users who query Teradata must have Spool space allocated. The defined Spool amount for a user is a shared resource. As a user's Spool accumulates across all of their sessions, the Spool utilization may exceed the user's defined limit. When this occurs, the youngest request will abort, releasing its Spool to the other running sessions, and an error message is returned to the user. To minimize this occurrence, Teradata will automatically release Spool whenever it is no longer required for the processing of the request, or when the request has completed.

Spool space is allocated from the unused Perm space on a Teradata system. However, Spool space works differently from Perm space in that it can be allocated from any available space on the system (it does not require inheritance). Like Perm space, Spool space availability is limited to the amount available to the AMPs. Once the AMP runs out of Perm space, there will be no Spool available.

Figure 4.7 shows how Perm and Spool might exist on a 1 terabyte, 10 AMP, Teradata system:

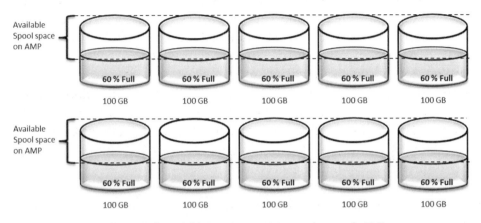

40% of available Perm space is unused on each AMP.
A total of 400 GB is currently available for Spool.

Figure 4.7

Temporary (Temp) Space

Temporary (Temp) space is disk space that is available for use in Global Temporary Tables. A user can use Temp space to populate data into their pre-defined Global Temporary Tables. When the user logs off their session, the data is purged from the Global Temporary Table and its hold on the space is released.

Like Spool space, Temp space comes from the unused Perm space on a Teradata system. Temp space can also be allocated from any available space on the system, and does not involve inheritance. Like Perm and Spool space, a Temp space definition is divided by the number of AMPs to provide a per-AMP limit. Once the AMP runs out of Perm space, there will be no Temp space available.

Teradata Connectivity

Mainframe Connections

Hardware

To connect to Teradata from a mainframe, a physical connection is required. A mainframe can either connect directly using an ESCON connection or using BUS/TAG cables, and then to a Host Channel Adapter. The Host Channel Adapter connects to a dedicated Parsing Engine (PE).

Software

The mainframe connects (via utilities, such as BTEQ, or other applications) to the CLIv2 and the Teradata Director Program (TDP). The CLIv2 issues commands directly to Teradata, and is responsible for request and response control, parcel creation and blocking/unblocking, buffer allocation and initialization. The TDP provides Teradata with information about the client so that it knows how to properly format the result set for the client and it handles session balancing and failure notification.

Channel Attached Configuration

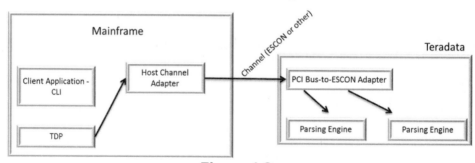

Figure 4.8

Local Area Network Connections

To make a successful connection between Teradata and a PC on the Local Area Network (LAN), both hardware and software components are required.

Hardware

An Ethernet network interface card is required to allow a computer to connect to the network, on both the Teradata system and each client PC.

Client Software

The CLIv2 (Call Level Interface) issues commands directly to Teradata and handles blocking/unblocking requests. The MOSI (Micro Operating System Interface) is a library of routines that handle the operating system and the networking interface. The MTDP (Micro Teradata Director Program) is a library of session management routines, ported for the specific operating system, and is linked into applications running on the network host. Finally, ODBC, JDBC, and OLE DB drivers are used to communicate from the client PC to the MTDP.

Teradata Software

The Gateway controls access between the LAN computers and Teradata. The Gateway controls user logons and can enable or disable user access. On the Teradata node, the AMP, PE, and PDE (Parallel Database Extensions) software handle the data request and retrieval.

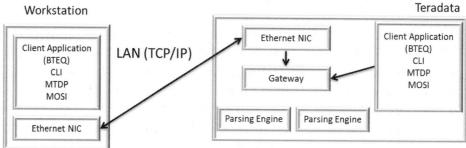

LAN Attached Configuration

Figure 4.9

Application Programming Interfaces (APIs)

ODBC

The most common way to connect to Teradata is via ODBC (Open Database Connectivity). ODBC is a standard software API, supported by most operating systems. In addition, ODBC is supported by most RDBMS systems, making it one of the more popular connection methods. Most query tools, including Teradata's SQL Assistant, support ODBC.

OLE DB

Another popular method of connecting to Teradata is via OLE DB (Object Linking and Embedding). Created by Microsoft, OLE DB is a standard software API, supported by most operating systems and by most RDBMS systems. While some query tools support OLE DB, it is most often used by ETL, program code, and other software applications.

JDBC

When programming in a Java/J2EE environment, the recommended connectivity method is the Teradata JDBC (Java Database Connectivity) driver. The Teradata JDBC driver is fully managed code and is written in Java.

Call Level Interface (CLIv2)

The Teradata Call Level Interface (CLI), also known as CLIv2, is a collection of callable routines that speak natively to Teradata, and can be invoked by outside applications. Because the CLIv2 speaks directly to Teradata, it is an extremely efficient mode of communication. The CLI allows applications and users on both LAN and mainframe attached systems to communicate with Teradata directly, rather than using ODBC, OLE DB, or other protocols.

Chapter 4: Practice Questions

1. Which user is the master user?
   - A. ABC
   - B. CDC
   - C. DCB
   - D. DBC

2. Which layer parses SQL code?
   - A. AMP
   - B. Bynet
   - C. PE
   - D. Vdisk

3. Which layer routes commands and data to their proper destination?
   - A. AMP
   - B. Bynet
   - C. PE
   - D. Vdisk

4. Which layer stores, retrieves, and processes data?
   - A. AMP
   - B. Bynet
   - C. PE
   - D. Vdisk

5. Which of the following is not a Teradata space definition?
   - A. Disk space
   - B. Permanent space
   - C. Spool space
   - D. Temporary Space
   - E. Virtual space

6. Which of the following is responsible for handling blocking/unblocking requests?
    A. MTDP
    B. MOSI
    C. LAN
    D. CLI

Chapter Notes

Utilize this space for notes, key points to remember, diagrams, areas of further study, etc.

_____

_____

_____

_____

_____

_____

_____

_____

_____

_____

_____

_____

_____

_____

_____

_____

_____

_____

_____

_____

_____

Chapter 5: Database Managed Storage and Data Access

Certification Objectives

- ✓ Explain the effects of the Primary Index on data distribution and organization.
- ✓ Explain the effects of No Primary Index on data distribution and organization.
- ✓ Describe the differences between Primary Index and Primary Key.
- ✓ Describe the differences between non-partitioned, single level, and multi-level partitioned tables.
- ✓ Identify the differences between Columnar and Row storage.
- ✓ State the reasons for defining a UPI (Unique Primary Index) vs. a NUPI (Non-Unique Primary Index).
- ✓ State the reasons for defining a USI (Unique Secondary Index) vs. a NUSI (Non-Unique Secondary Index).
- ✓ Identify the reasons for using a primary index versus no primary index.
- ✓ Describe the trade-offs between Index access and Full Table Scans.
- ✓ Describe the operation and/or causes of Full Table Scans.
- ✓ State the reasons for defining a PPI (Partitioned Primary Index) and/or Multi-level Partitioned Primary Index.
- ✓ Describe the benefits of join indexes.
- ✓ List the types, levels, and functionality of locking provided by Teradata.
- ✓ Identify the reasons for choosing between Columnar and row storage.

Before You Begin

You should be familiar with the following terms and concepts.

Terms	Key Concepts
Primary Indexes and Data Distribution	Understanding UPI, NUPI, PPI, and MLPPI
Secondary Indexes	Utilizing USI, and NUSI for query performance
Join Indexes	Single table, multi-table, and aggregate
Locking	Types and levels of locks
No Primary Index	Distribution and uses

Data Distribution Management

Data distribution is managed automatically by the Teradata Database. The database administrators (DBAs) are not required to perform onerous data re-organizations. In addition, no complicated indexing schemes are needed to guarantee that the data is evenly distributed. Data is distributed automatically, based upon each table's specified Primary Index.

Primary Indexes

All tables must have at least one column specified as a Primary Index. The Primary Index is specified at table creation and can never be changed without dropping and recreating the entire table. A table may not have more than one Primary Index, but the index may consist of one or more columns, with a maximum of 64 columns.

The Primary Index is pivotal to Teradata tables, for the following reasons:

Data Distribution

The selection of the Primary Index columns directly determines the distribution of the table's rows. Ideally, the rows should be distributed as evenly as possible across the AMPs, so a Primary Index that guarantees good distribution should be carefully considered. If distribution is poor, the performance will suffer during full table scan operations because only a portion of Teradata's AMPs are busy processing data.

Data Retrieval

The Primary Index is the fastest way to retrieve data. Because all data is distributed according to the Primary Index, it will physically provide the quickest route to the data because it will always be a one AMP operation.

Join Performance

The Primary Index can significantly impact the performance of query joins.

Primary Index and Primary Key

A Primary Index is different from a primary key in that its values can be non-unique, its values can change, and its purpose is not for row identification, but rather for data distribution.

The Primary Index is often, but not necessarily the same column(s) as the primary key. This is because the Primary Index is designed to be the best physical path to the data, whereas the primary key is intended to be a unique identifier. The Primary Index, by design, maximizes performance and accessibility.

Unique Primary Index (UPI)

In a Unique Primary Index (UPI), all values in the Primary Index column(s) must be unique, with no duplicate values in any other row in the table. Any row inserted with a duplicate value in the Primary Index column will be rejected. Note, for multi-column Unique Primary Indexes, each individual column may be non-unique, but the data values in the column combination must always be unique.

The UPI will evenly distribute the rows across all the AMPs. Therefore, a UPI is usually the best type of Primary Index to select when creating a table. The UPI also ensures that data is retrieved on the fastest physical path because a UPI accesses the data as a one AMP operation, and no duplicate row checks are performed.

In Figure 5.1, you will see that the CUST_ID column has been selected as the Unique Primary Index.

Table: CUSTOMER, with UPI on CUST_ID

CUST_ID	AREA	LAST_NM	FIRST_NM
333	3	Roark	Oscar
369	4	Gatsby	Walter
665	2	Mendoza	Manny

Figure 5.1

Non-Unique Primary Index (NUPI)

In a Non-Unique Primary Index (NUPI) the values in the Primary Index column(s) are NOT required to be unique. A NUPI may consist of one or more columns. In a NUPI, duplicate values in other table rows are allowed. Because duplicate values are allowed and they may occur frequently, the NUPI will not evenly distribute the rows across all the AMPs. However, based on the number of duplicate values, the quality of the data distribution will vary (less duplicate values equal better data distribution).

Because of the duplicate values, the NUPI is usually a less efficient type of Primary Index than the UPI. However, even though the NUPI is not evenly distributed, it can still be a very effective way to retrieve data and NUPIs are very efficient for query access and joins along with being a one AMP operation.

In Figure 5.2, you will see that the LAST_NM column has been selected as the Non-Unique Primary Index, and that duplicate values exist in the column.

Table: CUSTOMER, with NUPI on LAST_NM

CUST_ID	AREA	LAST_NM	FIRST_NM
333	3	Roark	Oscar
345	1	Roark	Carol
369	4	Gatsby	Walter
665	2	Mendoza	Manny

Figure 5.2

Default Primary Index

When you issue a CREATE TABLE statement, the system examines the syntax and the DBS Control parameter DefaultPrimaryIndex to see if it's set to D, P, or N. The CREATE TABLE syntax, and the setting of that parameter, will control whether the table is created with a Primary Index. The following chart describes how the system decides.

IF . . .	THEN . . .
The table is a temporal table	Temporal must be Multiset and have an explicit NUPI.
The table has an explicit NO PRIMARY INDEX clause	Create a Multiset table with NO PRIMARY INDEX.
The table has column partitioning	Create a Multiset table with NO PRIMARY INDEX.
The table has an explicit UPI or NUPI	Create the table with the defined index.
There is no Primary Index clause, but there is a PK defined	Then create the table with a UPI on the PK column set
There is no Primary Index clause, no PK, but there is a UNIQUE constraint	Then create the table with a UPI on the first UNIQUE constraint.
There is no Primary Index clause, no PK, no UNIQUE constraint, and the DefaultPrimaryIndex = D or P	Then create the table with a NUPI on the first column.
There is no Primary Index clause, no PK, no UNIQUE constraint, and the DefaultPrimaryIndex = N	Then create the table with NO PRIMARY INDEX.

Figure 5.3

Primary Index vs. No Primary Index

Except for unpartitioned NoPI tables, column-partitioned tables and join indexes, and global temporary trace tables, each Teradata Database table, hash, and join index must have a primary index.

The primary use of an unpartitioned NoPI table is as a staging table for FastLoad, and Teradata Parallel Data Pump Array INSERT data loading operations for both unpartitioned and column-partitioned tables.

Because there is no primary index for the rows of a NoPI table, its rows are not hashed to an AMP based on their primary index value.

Instead, Teradata Database either hashes on the Query ID for a row, or uses a different algorithm to assign the row to its home AMP.

Teradata Database then generates a RowID for each row in a NoPI table by using a hash bucket that an AMP owns and using it to generate a RowID. This strategy makes fallback and index maintenance very similar to their maintenance on a PI table.

Partitioned Primary Index (PPI)

The Primary Index is designed to distribute the data evenly across the AMPs. However, the data may not be distributed in such a way that is conducive to user data requests. A table can be distributed across all the AMPs, with no regard to how that data should be logically ordered. On Primary Index columns that have range-based data, such as date values, Teradata is often forced to perform a Full Table Scan to retrieve all the dates within the SQL statement's specified range.

To solve this data management problem, Teradata has the Partitioned Primary Index (PPI), which specifies how the user wants the table data to be physically organized on the AMPs, within the Primary Index. The data will still be distributed across all AMPs, but the specified data ranges will be grouped together on each AMP. The partition is defined within the Primary Index declaration in the table's DDL statement.

There are several advantages of using a PPI versus a table without a PPI (which is referred to as a "non-partitioned table" or a "NPPI"). When a query is submitted, Teradata will have a much easier time locating the data, since the PPI is ordered with the data in mind, thus reducing the likelihood of a Full Table Scan. Using partition elimination, the Optimizer can avoid entire partitions of data that are not within the range of the partition column, within the requested answer set. Finally, PPIs allow for the rapid deletion and insertion of data. PPIs yield the biggest performance on large tables, but the SQL statement must always include the range constraint.

Multi-Level Partitioned Primary Index (MLPPI)

A Multi-Level Partitioned Primary Index (MLPPI) allows a partition to be sub-partitioned. A Single-Level PPI is only one-level deep; in that only a single range or case expression is partitioned. In a MLPPI, additional partition expressions can be specified, which provides the Optimizer with additional access paths to the data. The Optimizer utilizes the additional partition expressions to further pinpoint the targeted data, through enhanced partition elimination. A MLPPI must have at least two specified partitions.

For instance, a table that has a MLPPI on sales date and area code can help improve the performance on queries that commonly search for sales, during a specified timeframe, within different area codes. Using partition elimination, the Optimizer scans through only the data on the AMPs that fall within the date range, and within the specified area codes.

Secondary Indexes

Primary Indexes are the quickest path to data, but only a single Primary Index can exist on a table. However, there are often other, equally important, columns on a table which are repeatedly accessed (WHERE clauses). Because they are not specified as the Primary Index columns, the Optimizer often will choose to perform a Full Table Scan to return the result set.

Defining a Secondary Index will help to address these scenarios. A Secondary Index is similar to a Primary Index, in that it provides a path to the data. It improves the performance of individual queries and decreases the overall burden on Teradata by avoiding Full Table Scans. A Secondary Index is very useful in situations where table joining, aggregations, value comparisons, complex conditions, and character matching are required.

However, the Secondary Index operates quite differently than the Primary Index. The Secondary Index does NOT determine how rows are distributed across the AMPs. The column values of the Secondary Index are stored in a sub-table, which is spread across all AMPs. In addition, Secondary Indexes require both disk space and maintenance. Unlike the Primary Index, the Secondary Index is optional, and it does not have to be implemented at table creation. Secondary Indexes can be added and dropped, as necessary.

Figure 5.4 provides a quick reference to how the Primary and Secondary Indexes compare:

Primary Index vs. Secondary Index

	Primary Index	Secondary Index
Required	Yes	No
Can be unique or non-unique	Yes	Yes
Used for row distribution	Yes	No
Create and drop dynamically	No	Yes
Improves access	Yes	Yes
Create using multiple data types	Yes	Yes
Requires separate physical structure	No	Yes (subtable)
Requires extra processing overhead	No	Yes

Figure 5.4

Similar to the Primary Index, the Secondary Index allows for two different types of indexes: the Unique Secondary Index (USI) and the Non-Unique Secondary Index (NUSI).

Unique Secondary Index (USI)

A Unique Secondary Index (USI) must only contain unique values. The USI is efficient because the uniqueness ensures that Teradata can easily identify whether the SQL requested value even exists, by checking the Optimizer to see if any AMP carries the requested value. A Unique Secondary Index is also excellent for enforcing a primary key's uniqueness constraint. The USI is a two AMP operation, which is a significant improvement over an all AMP, Full Table Scan.

Non-Unique Secondary Index (NUSI)

Non-Unique Secondary Indexes (NUSIs) are often created on columns that are commonly queried and have reoccurring, non-unique, column values. The NUSI is an all AMP-local operation because every AMP has a Secondary Index sub-table that points to its own base rows.

When an SQL statement is executed with a NUSI column in the WHERE clause, the Parsing Engine directs all AMPs to check their sub-tables for matching rows. Each AMP will respond back with its rows, or indicate that it has none to return. Although each AMP is accessed, this is still much faster than a Full Table Scan, because the sub-table points directly to the requested rows.

Join Index (JI)

A Join Index (JI) is comprised of simple or aggregated information, from one or more tables. Join Indexes can significantly improve performance by storing information that is commonly joined or aggregated by user queries. Join Indexes are physical and require permanent space. A Join Index is automatically updated whenever the base table is updated.

The Teradata Optimizer will evaluate its options and determine whether to retrieve data from the base data or the Join Index. A Join

Index is beneficial because it can avoid the need to access the base table or to perform aggregate processing. If more than one table is used by the JI, costly table joins and redistributions can be avoided, as well.

Based on how the Join Index is structured, it can be classified as a Single Table Join Index, Multi-Table Join Index, or Aggregate Join Index.

Single Table Join Index (STJI)

An STJI is the simplest type of Join Index. It is comprised only of rows from a single table. It provides an alternate and more efficient access path for the Optimizer, rather than the Primary Index, when joining to another table. The STJI can accomplish the join by accessing the data directly, without the redistribution of data across the AMPs.

Multi-Table Join Index (MTJI)

An MTJI is a Join Index that consists of two or more tables. The MTJI contains the result data for matched join columns. The Optimizer can use the MTJI, rather than the actual table joins, to more quickly and effectively return the data.

Aggregate Join Index (AJI)

Like an MTJI, an AJI can also consist of one or more tables. However, an AJI is different from an STJI and MTJI in that some of the columns in the Join Index are actually aggregations of data, rather than just the base table data. By pre-aggregating the data, the AJI helps to avoid the repeated aggregation of commonly executed calculations. This can be an extremely cost effective method of increasing query performance. An AJI can be used for SUM, AVERAGE, and COUNT functions.

Teradata Columnar

The Teradata Columnar feature consists of integrated column partitioning, columnar storage, autocompression, as well as other supporting capabilities that you can specify for No Primary Index (NoPI) tables and single-table, nonaggregate, noncompressed NoPI join indexes.

Column partitioning stores single columns or sets of columns from a NoPI table or NoPI join index in separate partitions. You can store data in a column partition using either traditional row storage or columnar storage. Columnar storage packs the values of a column partition into a series of containers, significantly reducing the number of row headers that would otherwise be required.

Teradata Database automatically detects and applies opportunities for autocompression. You can partition a NoPI table by column, by row, or both by using multilevel partitioning. The primary use for a column-partitioned table or join index occurs when table or row partitions are loaded with an INSERT...SELECT request and used to run analytics or data mining.

Teradata columnar permits efficient access to selected data through the use of secondary indexes, which reduces query I/O. It adds flexibility in defining a partitioned table or join index. Such flexibility provides opportunities to improve workload performance. It also enables the optimizer to exclude unneeded column partitions, significantly enhancing query performance.

Figure 5.5 shows a normal row partitioned NoPI table with four data rows.

CREATE MULTISET TABLE nopi1
(A CHAR(20)
,B CHAR(20)
,C CHAR(20)
,D CHAR(20)
)
NO PRIMARY INDEX;

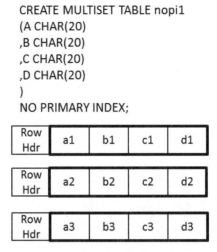

Figure 5.5

Figure 5.6 shows the same table column partitioned on the individual columns.

CREATE MULTISET TABLE nopi1
(A CHAR(20)
,B CHAR(20)
,C CHAR(20)
,D CHAR(20)
)
NO PRIMARY INDEX
PARTITION BY COLUMN;

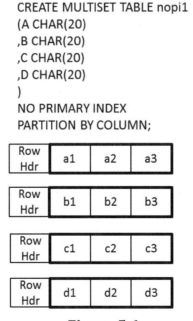

Figure 5.6

Index Columns and Statistics

Statistics can be collected at either the index or column level, and should be refreshed whenever the rows in the table significantly change. To ensure that the Optimizer has the best information possible, it is recommended that you always collect statistics on index columns. If statistics are not collected, or stale, the Optimizer may choose to perform a Full Table Scan, which may significantly decrease performance.

Data Distribution on the AMPs

The Primary Index ensures that data is distributed across each AMP on the Teradata system. Therefore, every AMP must also hold a portion of a every table's data. Figure 5.7 illustrates a sample 4 AMP Teradata system with three tables. The data for each table exists on each AMP with the data spread as evenly as possible.

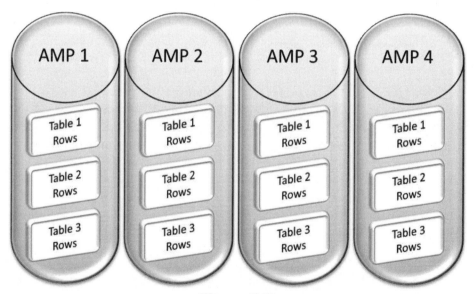

Figure 5.7

Teradata 14 Certification Study Guide

Unique Primary Indexes will always have good table distribution across all AMPs. This is because all the values are unique, and can therefore be distributed consistently without Teradata having to group duplicate hashed index values on the same AMP. In the following example, table Customer has a UPI of CUST_ID. Since each value in the Primary Index column must be unique, the data is evenly distributed across all AMPs, as seen in Figure 5.8.

AMP Distribution for Customer Table

Figure 5.8

Figure 5.9, table Shipping_Status has a NUPI on Shipping Status Code. Since only two values exist for shipping status ("yes" or "no"), you see that only two AMPs are actually used for storing this data. This will result in an uneven data distribution, and should be avoided. A Primary Index should only be chosen with columns that have a wide range of hashed values, in order to avoid data skewing on the AMPs.

AMP Distribution for Shipping_Status Table

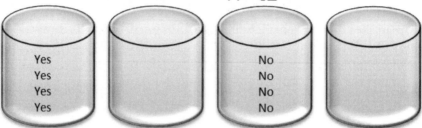

Figure 5.9

Figure 5.10, table Customer_Payments, has a NUPI on payment date. Many different payment dates can occur, and the data is distributed (as evenly as possible) across all of the AMPs, according to their hashed values.

AMP Distribution for Customer_Payments Table

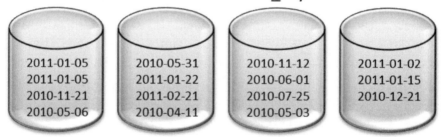

Figure 5.10

Access Methods

The Optimizer has its choice among different data access methods to retrieve the data on the AMPs. It evaluates each choice and selects the method which it determines to be the most efficient for the particular request.

Primary Index

The Primary Index is the most efficient way to retrieve data. Because the Primary Index points directly to the AMP where the data is located, the Optimizer knows exactly where to go to get the data. This is the fastest method, but the Primary Index column(s) must be specified in the search criteria in order to leverage this access path.

Secondary Index

If a Secondary Index exists on the table, and if the Optimizer determines that the Primary Index cannot be used, then the Secondary Index will be used to retrieve the data. This is the second fastest method for retrieving data but it requires that the Secondary Index column(s) appear within the query's search criteria.

Full Table Scan

When neither the Primary nor Secondary Indexes are specified as the access path, the Optimizer will request a Full Table Scan (FTS) to be performed against the entire table. When an FTS occurs, Teradata utilizes its parallelism capabilities to simultaneously retrieve the data from all of the AMPs. Because of parallelism, this may be the fastest method for accessing the data, if other access methods are determined to take longer than the FTS.

An FTS typically occurs when the user does not specify a Primary or Secondary Index column in their WHERE clause or if a Secondary

Index is not strongly selective. However, it may also occur when a non-equality clause is used on an index column, or when a range of values is specified on an index column. In addition, if many duplicates occur within a non-unique index, the Optimizer may determine that an FTS is the most efficient way to sort through the data. Finally, the Optimizer may choose to perform an FTS if it determines that it is the most direct access path, which can occur if the table contains a very small number of rows.

The best way to avoid an FTS is to specify a value for each column in the Primary or Secondary Index, which increases the likelihood that the Optimizer will choose the index as its preferred access method. Ensuring that the Primary and Secondary Index columns are fairly unique also helps to ensure that the index columns will be chosen. The Primary Index determines data distribution but can also be useful in defining the best path to the data. However, because a Primary Index does not always translate into the best (or all conceivable) access paths, you can create Secondary Indexes that provide direct paths to the data. Finally, collecting index and column statistics, and refreshing the statistics as the data changes will also help to ensure that the Optimizer has the information it needs to determine the best access path.

Locking

Purpose of Locks

A lock is used to assert a type of privilege on an object in the Teradata Database, such as a database, table, view, or specific row(s) of data. Locks are used to guarantee data integrity during the execution of simultaneous and conflicting user requests. There are four different types of locks: exclusive, write, read, and access; each lock varies in its abilities and priorities.

Types of Locks

Exclusive

Exclusive locks are the most powerful and restrictive of all locks. They are applied at the database or table level (not the row level), and are automatically applied when performing a Data Definition Language (DDL) command, such as a CREATE or ALTER command. When an exclusive lock is applied, no other user request can access the locked database or table until the lock has been released. No other lock can be placed on the locked database or table, not even an access lock.

Write

Write locks help maintain data consistency while data is being updated. When a write lock is placed on the data, a user is not able to place any other type of lock on the data, except for an access lock.

Read

Read locks help to ensure that the data is not changed, guaranteeing data consistency, while the read operation is being performed. Read locks are compatible with other read locks. Exclusive and write locks cannot be placed on the data until the read lock has been released. However, an access lock can still be used.

Access

Access locks are used to allow a user to read data, even while the data is locked for read or write. Access locks are used when the user is not concerned with complete data accuracy. Access locks help to improve query response time, since the user is not forced to wait until other locks have been freed. When an access lock is used, an exclusive lock may not be granted to another user until the access lock has been released.

Locking Levels

Teradata supports different levels of locking, to ensure that the appropriate objects and rows of data are locked, based upon the requested lock.

Database

The lock is applied to all tables, views, macros and triggers within the database/user. This level of locking is the widest approach, locking the largest number of objects and data. This lock is useful when processing large amounts of data, across many objects.

Table/View

The lock is applied to all rows in the table, and to all tables referenced in a view. This lock is useful when working with large amounts of data, within a single table or set of tables.

Row

The lock is applied to one or more rows in a table, based upon the row hash. This lock helps to improve performance by minimizing the amount of data that is locked from other user requests.

Chapter 5: Practice Questions

1. Which statement about Join Indexes is false?
   A. Can be directly selected by the user in a query
   B. Can be comprised of one or more tables
   C. May only consist of a single column
   D. Require Permanent space
   E. May contain simple or aggregated data

2. Which statement is true about column partitioned (columnar) tables?
   A. They must be SET tables with a UPI
   B. They must be a MULTISET table with a NUPI
   C. They must be a SET table with a NUPI
   D. They must be a MULTISET table with a UPI
   E. They must be a SET table with NoPI
   F. They must be a MULTISET table with NoPI

3. Which statement is false?
   A. Data tables may be both row and column partitioned
   B. Data tables may be either column partitioned or row partitioned, but not both
   C. Column partitioned tables may have secondary indexes
   D. Aggregate join indexes may not be column partitioned

4. What is designed to be the best unique identifier?
   A. Primary Index
   B. Secondary Index
   C. Primary Key
   D. Foreign Key

5. What is the best physical path to data?
    A. Primary Index
    B. Secondary Index
    C. Primary Key
    D. Foreign Key

6. Which index requires a separate physical structure?
    A. Primary Index
    B. Partitioned Primary Index
    C. Multi-level Partitioned Primary Index
    D. Secondary Index

7. Which statement about column-partitioned tables is true?
    A. The table must be a multiset table with NoPI
    B. The table must be a multiset table with a NUPI
    C. The table must be a set table with NoPI
    D. The table must be a set table with a NUPI

8. Which is the least restrictive lock?
    A. Access
    B. Exclusive
    C. Read
    D. Write

Chapter Notes

Utilize this space for notes, key points to remember, diagrams, areas of further study, etc.

Chapter 6: Storage Optimization

Certification Objectives

- ✓ Describe the concept of multi-temperature data.
- ✓ Identify the storage optimization techniques that exist in Teradata.

Before You Begin

You should be familiar with the following terms and concepts.

Terms	Key Concepts
Compression	Lossy and Lossless

Compression

Compression reduces the physical size of stored information. The goal of compression is to represent information accurately using the fewest number of bits. Compression methods are either logical or physical. Physical data compression re-encodes information independently of its meaning, while logical data compression substitutes one set of data with another, more compact set.

Most forms of compression are transparent to applications, ETL utilities, and queries. This can be less true of algorithmic compression, because a poorly performing decompression algorithm can have a negative effect on system performance, and in some cases a poorly written decompression algorithm can even corrupt data.

Compression enhances system performance because there is less physical data to retrieve per row for queries. Also, because compressed data remains compressed while in memory, the FSG cache can hold more rows, reducing the size of disk I/O.

Teradata Database uses several types of compression

FOR this database element ...	Compression refers to ...
Column values	Either multi-value or algorithmic compression
Hash and join indexes	Row compression
Data blocks	Block-level compression
Containers	The autocompression method set determined by Teradata Database to apply to a container of a column-partitioned table or join index.

Figure 6.1

Lossy and Lossless Compression

Lossy compression is a data encoding method that compresses data by discarding (losing) some of it. Lossy compression is most commonly used to compress multimedia data (audio, video, and still images).

By contrast, lossless compression is required for text and numerical data.

Row compression, multi-value compression, block-level compression, and autocompression are lossless methods, meaning that the original data can be reconstructed exactly from the compressed forms, while algorithmic compression can be either lossless or lossy, depending on the algorithm used.

Multi-Value Compression (MVC)

The system copies the compressible values, from the CREATE/ALTER TABLE statement, into the table header on every AMP. It then sets the Presence Bits for each row to indicate the status of each column: NULL or NOT NULL, not compressed, COMPRESSed on NULL, COMPRESSed on a specific data value from the list in the table header.

While multi-value compression removes specified values from row storage, those values do not disappear: they must be stored somewhere. This statement applies only to values, not nulls. Null compression is handled by the presence bits in the row header and does not have an impact on the table header.

The presence bits in the row header are where the compressed values are stored - once per column per AMP. However, this does not apply to algorithmically compressed data, which is stored in place within the row.

Because the size of the table header is limited to 1 MB, there is a limit to how many bytes can be compressed for a given column. If the number of bytes compressed exceeds the maximum row length, then the CREATE or ALTER TABLE statement used to create the new table is not valid and the DDL statement aborts. This is true even if the number of values specified for compression does not exceed the upper limit of 255.

Figure 6.1 is an example of a table with Single and Multi-Value Compression. The column *street_2* compresses only nulls while the columns *city_name* and *state_code* compress multiple values.

Note: You can compress VARCHAR columns.

```
CREATE TABLE Customer_Address
(cust_id INTEGER NOT NULL
,address_id BYTEINT NOT NULL
,street_1 CHAR(30) NOT NULL
,street_2 CHAR(30) COMPRESS
,city_name VARCHAR(40) COMPRESS ('Chicago', 'Atlanta',
       'San Francisco', 'New York City', 'Denver') NOT NULL
,state_code CHAR(2) NOT NULL COMPRESS ('IL', 'CA', NY', 'GA',
       'CO')
,zip_code (CHAR(10) NOT NULL
)
PRIMARY INDEX (cust_id);
```

Figure 6.2

Row-Level Compression

If you know that a join index contains groups of rows with repeating information, then its Data Definition Language (DDL) can specify repeating groups, indicating the repeating columns within a separate set of parentheses from the fixed columns. In other words, the column list is specified as two groups of columns, with each group delimited within parentheses. The first group contains the repeating columns and the second group contains the fixed columns.

You cannot define both row compression and a row-partitioned primary index for the same join index.

When describing compression of join index rows, compression refers to a logical row compression in which multiple sets of non-repeating column values are appended to a single set of repeating column values. This allows Teradata Database to store the repeating value set only once, while any non-repeating column values are stored as logical segmental extensions of the base repeating set.

In the following Figure 6.2, the join index JIDX_1 does not specify any row compression, while the join index JIDX_2 identifies the first two columns should have duplicate values compressed and values for the remaining columns appended as segmental extensions.

```
CREATE JOIN INDEX JIDX_1 AS
SELECT c1, c2, c3, c4, c5
FROM t1
PRIMARY INDEX (c3);

CREATE JOIN INDEX JIDX_2 AS
SELECT (c1, c2), (c3, c4, c5)
FROM t2
PRIMARY INDEX (c3);
```

Figure 6.3

Columnar Container Compression

When you create a column-partitioned table or join index, Teradata Database attempts to use one or more methods to compress the data that you insert into the physical rows of the object unless you specify the NO AUTO COMPRESS option at the time you create it. The process of selecting and applying appropriate compression methods to the physical containers of a column-partitioned table or join index is referred to as *autocompression*.

Note: Autocompression is most effective for a column partition with a single column and COLUMN format.

Teradata Database only applies autocompression to column partitions with COLUMN format, and then only if it reduces the size of a container. Teradata Database autocompresses column partitions by default, with the following requirements:

- Minimal CPU resources are required to decompress the data for reading.
- Teradata Database does not need to decompress many values to find a single value.

Teradata Database applies autocompression for a physical row on a per container basis. This means that the containers in a column partition might be autocompressed in different ways. In most cases, the data type of a column is not a factor, and Teradata Database compresses values based only on their byte representation. As a general rule, the only difference that needs to be considered is whether the byte representation is fixed or variable length.

For some values, there are no applicable compression techniques that can reduce the size of the physical row, so Teradata Database does not compress the values for that physical row. However, the Teradata Database does attempt to compress physical row values using one of the autocompression methods available to it. When you retrieve rows from a column-partitioned table, Teradata Database automatically decompresses any compressed column partition values as is necessary.

Algorithmic Compression (ALC)

In algorithmic compression, you use scalar UDFs to compress and decompress byte, character, or graphic data values. You determine the compression and decompression algorithms. You must specify a decompression algorithm when you create or alter the table that contains the compressed column data.

Depending on the implementation, algorithmic compression can be either physical or logical, though most implementations use physical data compression. Algorithmic compression can be either lossy or lossless, depending on the algorithm used.

Algorithmic compression and multi-value compression can be used independently, or a column specification can contain both. In Figure 6.3, *c2* uses just ALC, *c3* uses just MVC, and *c4* will use MVC for three values and ALC for all other values.

```
CREATE TABLE mvc_alc
(c1 INTEGER NOT NULL
,c2 VARCHAR COMPRESS USING LZCOMP_L
            DECOMPRESS USING LZDECOMP_L
,c3 VARCHAR COMPRESS ('ABC', 'BCD', 'CDE')
,c4 VARCHAR COMPRESS ('DEF', 'EFG', 'FGH')
            COMPRESS USING LZCOMP_L
            DECOMPRESS USING LZDECOMP_L
)
PRIMARY INDEX (c1);
```

Figure 6.4

Block-Level Compression

Block-level compression enables any normal data block to be stored in compressed form. BLC applies to primary data tables, BLOB and CLOB subtables, fallback tables, join index subtables, hash index subtables, reference index subtables, spool tables, and journal tables, and is independent of any row compression, multi-value compression, or algorithmic compression applied to the same data. Block-level compression is a lossless method.

The goals of block-level compression are to save storage space and to reduce disk I/O bandwidth. While the number of physical I/O operations might be reduced by BLC, the number of logical I/O operations typically does not change. Block-level compression can use significantly more CPU to compress and decompress data dynamically, so whether query performance is enhanced with block-level compression depends on whether performance is more limited by disk I/O bandwidth or CPU usage. This level of compression is completely independent of any row compression, multi-value compression, or algorithmic compression applied to the same data.

Block-level compression is controlled by the Ferret utility, by several DBS Control parameters, or by the BlockCompression reserved query band.

Temperature-Based Block-Level Compression

Temperature-based block-level compression uses the temperature of data as maintained by Teradata Virtual Storage (TVS) to determine what to compress. For example, COLD or WARM data might be compressed automatically, while HOT data might be decompressed automatically if it was previously compressed.

Temperature-based block-level compression only applies to permanent user data tables.

When you issue a CREATE TABLE command, the BLOCKLEVELCOMPRESSION option controls the table's temperature-based block-level compression. The possible option values and their meaning are:

- AUTOTEMP - identifies tables whose temperature-based block-level compression state can be changed by the file system at any time based on its Teradata Virtual Storage temperature.

- DEFAULT - identifies tables whose temperature-based block-level compression is determined by the DBS Control parameter DefaultTableMode.

- MANUAL - identifies tables that are not managed automatically like AUTOTEMP tables are.

- NEVER - identifies tables that should never be block-level compressed, even if a query band or the applicable DBS Control parameter defaults indicate otherwise. The file system does not block-level compress the table and its subtables even if the DBS Control block compression settings indicate otherwise.

Teradata Virtual Storage tracks the cylinder temperature metrics for all tables when temperature-based block-level compression is enabled. Temperatures are in effect system-wide, and Teradata Virtual Storage takes all temperatures into account when it determines which data on a system is associated with which temperature.

Hardware-Based Block-Level Compression

In addition to software block-level compression, Teradata Database also offers hardware-based block-level compression for systems that have the required hardware. The advantage of hardware-based block-level compression is that compression and decompression of data presents very little CPU resource contention. Hardware-based block-level compression uses the Exar Corporation Lempel-Ziv-Stac algorithm.

Chapter 6: Practice Questions

1. The following DDL is an example of which form of compression?

   ```
   CREATE JOIN INDEX jdx_1 AS
   SELECT (col1, col2, col3), (col4, col5, col6)
   FROM t23
   PRIMARY INDEX (col4);
   ```

   A. ALC
   B. BLC
   C. Columnar
   D. MVC
   E. Row

2. The DDL term "NO AUTO COMPRESS" applies to which form of compression?
   A. ALC
   B. BLC
   C. Columnar
   D. MVC
   E. Row

3. Which of the following may be a lossy form of compression?
   A. ALC
   B. BLC
   C. Columnar
   D. MVC
   E. Row

4. Which type of compression may be based on the temperature of the data?
    A. ALC
    B. BLC
    C. Columnar
    D. MVC
    E. Row

5. Assuming there is sufficient space in the table header, what is the maximum number of distinct values that can be specified for compression in a single column?
    A. 63
    B. 127
    C. 255
    D. 511
    E. 1023

Chapter Notes

Utilize this space for notes, key points to remember, diagrams, areas of further study, etc.

_____

_____

_____

_____

_____

_____

_____

_____

_____

_____

_____

_____

_____

_____

_____

_____

_____

_____

_____

_____

_____

_____

Chapter 7: Data Availability Features

Certification Objectives

- ✓ Describe hardware specific data and performance protection techniques.
- ✓ Explain the concept of FALLBACK tables.
- ✓ Describe how Transient Journal ensures data integrity.
- ✓ Describe the concept of node failover.

Before You Begin

You should be familiar with the following terms and concepts.

Terms	Key Concepts
Transient Journal	Manages transactions and rollbacks
Fallback	Protects from AMP failures
Down AMP Journal	Supports data availability and recovery when an AMP fails
RAID 1, Cliques, and Hot Standby Nodes	Protects disk and nodes failures

Transient Journal

The primary responsibility of the Transient Journal is to keep a copy of the before images until either the transaction or rollback completes successfully. Once completed, the before images are discarded from the Transient Journal.

Figure 7.1 illustrates how the Transient Journal handles a row update. Remember, if the transaction is successful, the changes are committed. If the transaction fails, a rollback is performed, and the data is restored to its original state.

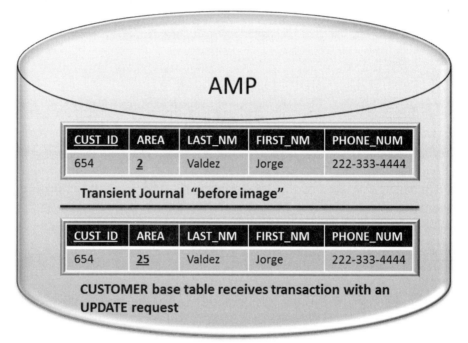

Figure 7.1

Specifically, the following occurs each time a SQL statement results in failure:

1) The submitting user receives an error message.
2) The transaction is rolled back and the data is returned to its original state.
3) Any locks are released.
4) All spool files associated with the request are released.

Note: the Transient Journal is an automatic Teradata process, and cannot be modified or disabled.

Fallback

Fallback is a data protection feature whose sole purpose is to avoid data loss during an AMP failure. If an AMP is lost due to a system failure, Fallback will ensure that a copy of the data exists on another AMP. Essentially, Fallback provides a duplicate copy of each row on the table.

The Fallback data is an exact copy and is updated concurrently from the primary data. Essentially, each data row has a twin image row on another AMP. Even though a mirror image can be said to exist, Fallback is not true data mirroring, because it spreads the duplicate rows across all of the AMPs in a cluster. Fallback can be specified at either the table or database level.

Figure 7.2 illustrates a simple table on a 4 AMP system. If a single AMP fails, Teradata will automatically switch over to the Fallback data. In this example, if an additional AMP fails, Teradata will stop processing, and since data integrity can no longer be assured. The following gives you a basic understanding of how Teradata organizes the rows across the AMPs within the same cluster.

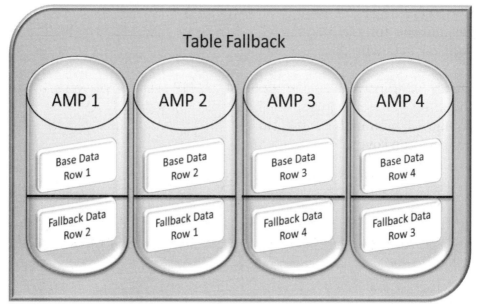

Figure 7.2

Fallback comes with a cost. Since the data is an exact copy, twice the amount of disk space is needed. Fallback is an optional feature; it can be turned on or off, based on the business need. When space is available, Fallback should be considered, due to its data-safekeeping ability.

Fallback Clusters

Fallback is a very powerful way to ensure data is duplicated and ready-to-go in the event of an AMP failure. However, when working with large Teradata systems, it is likely that there are numerous tables spread out across many AMPs. The more AMPs the system has, the greater potential for AMP failure. It is entirely possible to have multiple AMPs fail at the same time.

In the event of a multiple AMP failure, Fallback Clusters are used to mitigate the risk of data loss, as well as system downtime. Fallback

Clustering organizes groups of AMPs into clusters. Each cluster is responsible for maintaining all of the rows for its base table and Fallback data within the cluster.

Figure 7.3 illustrates clustering on an 8 AMP system. As you can see, the base table rows and their corresponding Fallback rows are contained within the same cluster. If one AMP fails in a cluster, Fallback can cover the missing AMP.

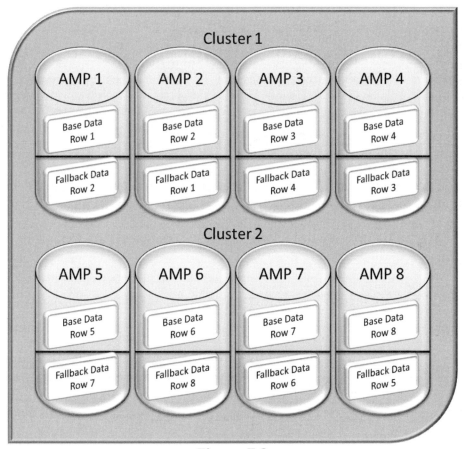

Figure 7.3

Down AMP Recovery Journal

The Down AMP Recovery Journal is used in the event of a down AMP when a table is Fallback protected. The journal starts up immediately and is used to keep track of all changes that are made to the data while the AMP is down. The journal is kept on all of the remaining AMPs in the cluster, since the Fallback data for the down AMP resides on their disks. The Recovery Journal is an automatic Teradata process, and cannot be modified or disabled.

The Recovery Journal is very similar to the Transient Journal, in that it keeps a log of all data changes that should have been made on the down AMP. The Recovery Journal is used to resynchronize the primary AMP when it is back online. The Recovery Journal is very useful because it prevents the need to completely rebuild the AMP's data from scratch when a failure occurs. Rather than rewriting all the data, only the missing transactions need to be applied. The Recovery Journal uses available Perm space to store its log. Once the AMP is restored and the data is resynchronized, the Recovery Journal is discarded and the Perm space is released. Figure 7.4 depicts a scenario where AMP 3 has failed:

OFFLINE

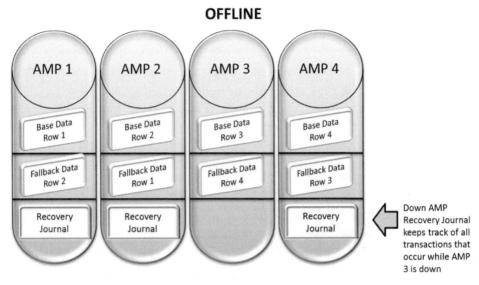

Figure 7.4

Redundant Array of Independent Disks (RAID)

Redundant Array of Independent Disks (RAID) is a technology that uses multiple disk drives to protect data from a single disk failure. All disks in a RAID configuration act as a single disk. The purpose of RAID is to ensure that, in the event of a disk failure, there is at least one more exact copy of the failed disk drive that is immediately available for use. In most cases, Teradata systems are pre-configured with RAID 1 as Figure 7.5 shows.

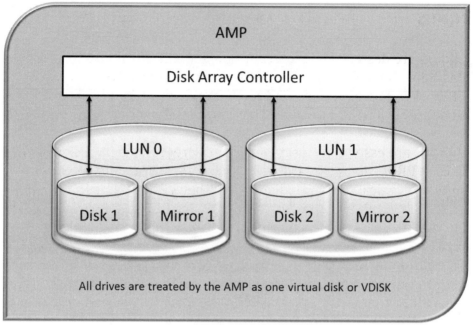

Figure 7.5

For Teradata systems, RAID 1 consists of two disks that are exact mirror images. The two disks are logically grouped and called a Logical Unit (LUN). The Operating System recognizes a LUN as a single, logical disk and is not aware that it is actually writing to spaces on multiple physical disk drives. When a mirror image fails, it does not impact the performance, space, or reliability of the remaining disk drives. Regardless of the number of mirror images, RAID 1 drives act as a single, virtual disk drive or VDISK. RAID 1 can require a significant amount of disk space, because an additional drive is required for every mirror image. A combination of RAID 1 and Fallback ensures that data is physically protected and fully redundant.

Cliques

Cliques are designed to protect Teradata in the event of a node failure. Basically Cliques are a mechanism that supports the migration of VPROCS following a node failure. If a node in a Clique fails, then that Node's VPROCS migrate to the other nodes in that Clique.

VPROCs are essentially a set of software processes that run on a node. Each VPROC is a separate, independent copy of the processor software, logically independent from other VPROCs, but sharing some of the physical resources of the node, such as memory and CPUs. Multiple VPROCs can run on a node.

Therefore, an AMP VPROC manages Teradata Database interactions with the disks. Each AMP manages its portion of the disk. The PE is the VPROC that communicates with the user system on one side and with the AMPs (via the BYNET) on the other side. Each PE executes the database software that manages sessions, breaks SQL statements into steps, possibly in parallel, and returns the query answer to the requesting user.

Figure 7.6, shows a Clique with four nodes. If a node fails, Teradata will temporarily reassign the VDISKs from the failed node to another node within the same Clique. In this case, all of the AMPs are migrated as evenly as possible across the remaining three nodes. The migrated AMPs can continue to perform read and write operations on the data stored on their VDISK. Cliques are pre-configured by Teradata, based on your specific hardware configuration.

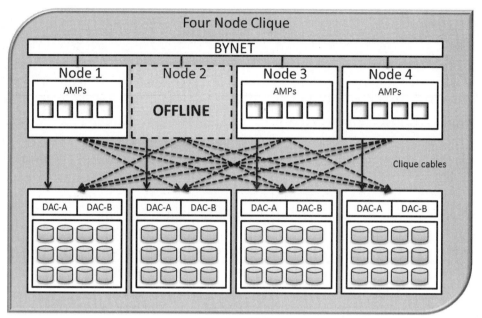

Figure 7.6

While the node is down, the AMPs can continue to perform read and write operations on the data contained on the virtual disks via the backup node. This will continue until the original node has been restored. Once restored, the AMPs migrate to their original node. Because a down node can result in a performance strain on the other nodes, Cliques work best on systems with multiple-node Clique configurations.

Hot Standby Node

A Hot Standby Node (HSN) is a backup node. It is a member of a clique, but does not normally participate in Teradata Database operations, see Figure 7.7 for an illustration. When a node fails, the AMPs from the failed node migrate to the Hot Standby Node. Hot Standby Nodes are positioned as a performance continuity feature. Therefore, the performance degradation is 0%.

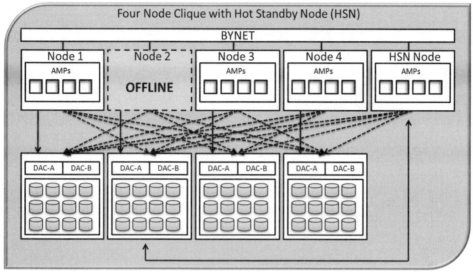

Figure 7.7

When the failed Node returns to service it becomes the "new" Hot Standby Node. Therefore, a second restart is not needed.

Note: Without a HSN, once a node is repaired it requires a restart to bring it back into the configuration. Because the HSN came into the configuration during the first restart, the repaired node now becomes the HSN and will rejoin the configuration on the next Teradata restart where a node fails.

Hot Standby Nodes have the following characteristics:

- They are member of a Clique.
- Are brought in to participate in Teradata Database operations when a node in the clique fails
- Can eliminate the system-wide performance degradation normally associated with the loss of a node.
- Eliminate the need to restart the system to bring the failed node into the configuration.

Chapter 7: Practice Questions

1. Which Teradata data protection mechanism can be disabled?
   A. Transient Journal
   B. Fallback
   C. Down AMP Recovery Journal
   D. RAID 1

2. Match the data protection to the failure it covers?
   A. RAID 1   1.   Node failure
   B. Transient Journal 2.   AMP failure
   C. Cliques   3.   Disk drive failure
   D. Fallback   4.   Transaction failure

3. "Hot Standby" is a term associated with _____.
   A. RAID 1
   B. Fallback
   C. Down AMP Recovery Journal
   D. Cliques

4. "Clusters" is a term associated with _____.
   A. RAID 1
   B. Fallback
   C. Down AMP Recovery Journal
   D. Cliques

5. Before images are kept by the _____.
   A. Down AMP Recovery Journal
   B. Transient Journal
   C. RAID 1
   D. Fallback

6. "Mirroring" is a term associated with _____.
   A. Cliques
   B. Fallback
   C. RAID 1
   D. Transient Journal

Chapter Notes

Utilize this space for notes, key points to remember, diagrams, areas of further study, etc.

_____

_____

_____

_____

_____

_____

_____

_____

_____

_____

_____

_____

_____

_____

_____

_____

_____

_____

_____

_____

_____

Chapter 8: Security and Privacy

Certification Objectives

- ✓ Identify security mechanisms available to Teradata.
- ✓ Identify privacy mechanisms available within Teradata.

Before You Begin

You should be familiar with the following terms and concepts.

Terms	Key Concepts
Access Rights	LDAP, and user privileges / rights
View and Macros	Data access methods
Stored Procedures and UDF	Conditional and procedural functions
Roles and Profiles	Administer and manage access rights

Authentication

One method to control access to the Teradata Database is by utilizing LDAP. LDAP (Lightweight Directory Access Protocol) provides a means of managing and centralizing user accounts in a network environment. LDAP offers a scalable and secure approach to network management. By utilizing this method, you can use LDAP to:

1. Authenticate users
2. Manage passwords
3. Supports a single sign-on strategy
4. Activate and deactivate accounts.

After users have been authenticated, they are then logged onto the Teradata Database. From there, they are authorized to access only those objects allowed by their database privileges.

Teradata Wallet

To avoid having to code their password in a .logon or .logdata statement, users can store usernames and passwords on a Teradata client computer or application server running Teradata Tools and Utilities 14.0 and up, using the included Teradata Wallet software, and then retrieve the needed data when logging on to the database.

Passwords and other data are securely stored in protected form. Each user can store data only in their own wallet, which is not accessible by other users. The system retrieves data only from the wallet belonging to the logged on user.

Users running scripted applications can embed password retrieval syntax into scripts instead of compromising security by including a password.

Users accessing multiple Teradata Database systems can automatically retrieve the correct username and password for a system (tdpid) instead of having to remember the information or look it up.

Once Teradata Wallet has been installed on your client system, do the following:

1. Logon to your client system.
2. At the command prompt, execute Teradata Wallet to create a password alias name:

```
tdwallet add <password_alias>
```

3. The software will prompt you to enter the password value for the alias name.

4. Then, reference your wallet in your script logon command.

```
.logon tdpid/username, $tdwallet (password_alias)
        [,"account "]
```

Privileges and Access Rights

Your privileges and access rights define the types of activities you can perform on an object when you are logged onto the Teradata Database. The following operations require that you have specific privileges and rights as outlined in Figure 8.1:

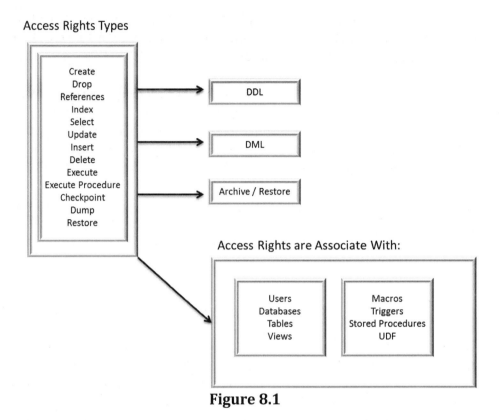

Figure 8.1

Privileges control user activities for manipulating database objects and data. This also includes the ability to grant access rights to other users in the database.

Access Rights Mechanisms

Access rights are categorized in one of three ways:

- Automatic (or Default) Access Rights - Automatic rights are privileges given to creators and, in the case of users and databases, their created objects. All rights are automatically removed for an object when it is dropped.

- Explicit Access Rights - Explicit rights are privileges conferred by using a GRANT statement. Explicit rights can be removed using the REVOKE statement.

- Implicit (or Ownership) Access Rights - Owners (Parents) have the implicit right to grant rights on any or all of their owned objects (Children), either to themselves or to any other user or database. Ownership rights cannot be taken away unless ownership is transferred.

In addition to access rights, Teradata Database implementations are typically configured so users only access tables or applications via the semantic layer. This would include Views, Macros, Stored Procedures, and UDFs.

Roles

Roles can be viewed as a collection of access rights, which can be granted to individual users or groups in order to protect the security of data and objects within the Teradata Database. Any user assigned a role – referred to as Granting a role – can access all of the objects the Role has rights to. A database administrator can create different roles for different job functions and responsibilities, grant specific privileges on database objects to these roles, and then grant these roles to users.

Advantages of Roles

Advantages of roles include:

- Simplify access rights administration
- Reduce disk space usage
- Improved performance

- Less dictionary contention during DDL operations because the commands use less time.

A database administrator can grant rights on database objects to a role. These rights are then automatically applied to all users assigned to that role. When a user's function within his organization changes, it is easier to change his/her role than deleting old rights and granting new rights that go along with the new function.

Profiles

With profiles, a database administrator can define a set of system parameters. Assigning a profile to a group of users ensures that all group members operate with a common set of parameters as outlined below:

- Default database
- Spool space capacity
- Temporary space capacity
- Account strings
- Password security attributes

To manage this common set of parameters, a database administrator can create a different profile for each user group, based on system parameters that group members share or require.

Profiles provide two primary advantages:

- Simplify administration of parameters
Easier control for user-level password security

Row Level Security

Access to Teradata Database objects, for example, tables and views is primarily based on object level user privileges. Object level privileges provide basic access control, but are discretionary, that is, object owners automatically have the right to grant access on any owned object to any other user.

In addition to object level privileges, you can use Teradata Row Level security to control user access for each table row, by SQL operation. Row level security access rules are based on the comparison of the access capabilities of each user and the row level security access requirements for each row.

Object owners do not have discretionary privileges to grant row access to other users. Only users with security constraint administrative privileges can manage row level access controls.

Government agencies commonly create security labels (classifications) and use them to define user access capabilities and row access requirements.

Implementation of row level security can be complicated compared to standard discretionary access controls. Before you commit to using row level security, determine whether or not you can meet access control needs by more conventional means. For example:

- Grant user access to views that do not include columns with sensitive data, instead of granting user privileges on the entire base table.
- Grant or revoke access privileges only on selected columns in the base table.

When comparing access control methods, consider that view and column level access controls:

- Are usually adequate for controlling SELECT statements, but users cannot execute INSERT, UPDATE, and DELETE statements on columns they cannot see, and must revert to accessing the base tables for these operations.
- Are discretionary, that is, the object owner can grant access to any user.

Views

A View is essentially a stored query that is accessible as a virtual table. Views, unlike tables, do not store data, but rather access data. Therefore, views are not physical entities and require no permanent space. However, they access actual table data using a SELECT statement. The SELECT statement is the main component of the view's definition, which is stored in the data dictionary. Underneath the covers, views fully leverage the massive parallel processing of Teradata. Views provide the following:

- Views can join together multiple tables to create a single virtual table. Views can help users to focus on getting the data they need, rather than spending substantial time writing SQL.

- Views can help to simplify data results. Many tables have complicated datasets that require aggregation and summarization before they are meaningful. Views are useful in performing these calculations behind the scenes.

- Views are useful because they can be written to exclude access to the sensitive columns, while providing access to the non-sensitive columns.

View Example

To create a view, you must specify a view name and the SQL statement. Views must be uniquely named, but only within their respective database/user.

In Figure 8.2, we create a simple view from our customer table. In this view, we are looking for all customers in area 2 whose policy amount is more than $500,000:

```
CREATE VIEW cust_area2_500plus_v AS
     SELECT cust_id
          , last_nm
          , first_nm
          , create_date
     FROM customer
     WHERE area = 2
        AND policy_amount > 500000;
```

Figure 8.2

Now that the view has been created, we can query the view. Suppose we want to further restrict the result set to only display customers who were created after the year 2011. Our new query looks like this:

```
SELECT * FROM cust_area2_500plus_v
WHERE create_date > '2011-12-31';
```

Figure 8.3

The results will now show all customers in area 2 with a policy amount greater than $500,000 and were created after 2011.

Macros

A Macro consists of one or more stored SQL statements, that when executed, are performed within a single transaction. Macros are often used to consolidate repetitive tasks and can also be used to perform complex operations. Macros, unlike tables, do not store data, but rather access data. Macros are therefore not physical entities and require no permanent space. Lastly, Macros reside in the data dictionary. Macros provide the following:

- They store SQL statements and common routines that save time that would otherwise be spent re-writing the same SQL and help reduce user SQL errors.

- They can be defined to receive input parameters from the user. The SQL statements can use the parameters as data values to allow for a parameterized query.

- They are also great for sharing. Macros are stored in the Data Dictionary and can be accessed by users that have been granted appropriate access.

Macro Example

As discussed, macros are even more powerful when they are designed to accept input parameters. A user can specify the parameter(s) at execution time which are consumed by the macro. The input parameters are plugged into the macro's pre-defined variables in the macro syntax and then the macro executes the SQL command(s). Macros may have one or more parameters.

To execute a macro with parameters, they must be specified, after the macro name, within parenthesis. Each parameter must have a name and an associated data type. Within the macro syntax, the variables must be prefaced with a colon ":".

In Figure 8.4, we create a "policy amount increase" macro. This time, we specify the area number as a parameter, so we can give policy amount increases at the area level.

```
CREATE MACRO GlobalPolicyIncreaseByArea
(inArea INTEGER) AS

(UPDATE customer
  SET policy_amount = policy_amount * 1.1
  WHERE  area = :inArea;

SELECT * FROM customer; );
```

Figure 8.4

When executed, this macro will increase all customer policy amounts, within the specified area, by ten percent.

Macro Execution

To use a macro, you must issue an EXECUTE statement, followed by the macro name and any required parameters as shown below.

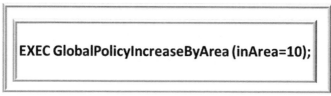

EXEC GlobalPolicyIncreaseByArea (inArea=10);

Figure 8.5

All parameters must be enclosed within parenthesis, following the macro name. If no parameters are required, then parentheses are not required.

Stored Procedures

A Stored Procedure is a set of SQL and procedural statements. Stored procedures are similar to programs. They are procedural, and they can receive input and return output. Although stored procedures share some of the same functionality with macros, there are differences which are outlined below:

- Both Macros and Stored Procedures contain SQL and can receive input. However, stored procedures require a small amount of physical storage.

- There are two types of stored procedures, internal and external. Typically stored procedures are internal, but Teradata allows for External Stored Procedures, which can be written in either Java™ or C++.

Note: External Stored Procedures do need to be compiled.

Stored procedures are also great for sharing because they are stored right on the database and can be accessed by as many users as necessary. Teradata has access rights which can be used to specify who can create, replace, drop, and execute the stored procedure.

Stored Procedure Example

Figure 8.6 is an example of a stored procedure. This procedure will delete the customer with the specified customer id from our Customer table:

```
CREATE PROCEDURE DeleteCustomer (IN inCust
INTEGER, OUT msg VARCHAR(20))

BEGIN

  DELETE FROM  customer
  WHERE cust_id = :inCust;
  SET msg = 'Delete Completed';

END;
```

Figure 8.6

Stored Procedure Execution

To execute a stored procedure, you must issue a CALL statement, followed by the stored procedure name and any required parameters.

In Figure 8.7, we execute our DeleteCustomer stored procedure. We pass in parameters of 100 and 200 (the two customer numbers) along with msg (which will return the message).

```
CALL DeleteCustomer(100, msg);
CALL DeleteCustomer(200, msg);
```

Figure 8.7

When executed, our stored procedure will return the message 'Delete Completed'.

User Defined Functions (UDFs)

A User Defined Function (UDF) is a function, which can perform calculations and complete SQL commands, and are invoked as expressions from within SQL statements. UDFs are stored in their parent database/user's permanent space.

Teradata UDFs can be scalar functions that return single values, aggregate functions that return summary tables and table functions that return tables. UDFs are written in Java, C, or C++ programming language.

UDFs are very useful for performing calculations and summarizations of data. The ability to program in Java, C, or C++ allows for extended programming capability, beyond that of SQL. Examples of UDFs might include a function that checks if a value is numeric or a function that converts Fahrenheit into Celsius.

Chapter 8: Practice Questions

1. Which of the following has no effect on security?
    A. Access rights
    B. Spool limits
    C. Profiles
    D. Roles
    E. Views

2. Which of the following allows you to avoid coding your password in a .logon statement?
    A. $billfold
    B. $purse
    C. $safe
    D. $wallet
    E. $wrapper

3. What is not a form of preventing unauthorized viewing of sensitive data?
    A. GRANT/REVOKE at the column level
    B. GRANT/REVOKE at the row level
    C. Create views which do not return all columns
    D. Create views which do not return all rows

4. Which statement is false?
    A. Object owners can grant/revoke row level security
    B. Row level security can be simulated using views
    C. You can grant/revoke access on selected columns
    D. View and column access control is discretionary

5. Which two can be written using C++? (Choose two)
    A. UDFs
    B. Macros
    C. Views
    D. Stored Procedures
    E. Roles

Chapter Notes

Utilize this space for notes, key points to remember, diagrams, areas of further study, etc.

Chapter 9: Teradata Tools and Utilities

Certification Objectives

- ✓ Identify the features and functions of data integration utilities.
- ✓ Identify the features and functions of the access tools available within the Teradata product suite.
- ✓ Identify the features and functions of the Teradata ARC utility.
- ✓ Identify the tools in the Teradata Analyst Pack.

Before You Begin

You should be familiar with the following terms and concepts.

Terms	Key Concepts
ETL Tools	Understanding BTEQ, FastExport, FastLoad, MultiLoad, TPump, and TPT
ARC	Backup and restoring options
Teradata Analyst Pack	Visual Explain, TSET. Index and Statistic Wizards

BTEQ

Basic Teradata Query (BTEQ) is a powerful and easy-to-use multipurpose utility that can be used in either a batch or interactive mode. BTEQ supports all types of SQL statements (INSERT / SELECT / DELETE / UPDATE), can create and utilize stored procedures, and execute certain Teradata commands. However, BTEQ is primarily used to do the following:

- **Data Loading** - BTEQ can load data directly from flat files. BTEQ can even read the output data directly from another

BTEQ job, using named pipes, without ever landing the data on a storage device.

- **Data Extraction** - BTEQ can create flat files from retrieved data (the output from a user's SELECT statement). BTEQ can also be used to provide the input data to another BTEQ job, using named pipes, without ever landing the data on a storage device.

- **Data Reporting** - BTEQ can create nicely formatted reports from retrieved data (the output from a user's SELECT statement). Data can be formatted and the reports can be designed with headers and footers.

FastLoad

FastLoad is a high performance data loading utility. FastLoad is the utility of choice when loading a large volume of data. FastLoad excels at reading flat files and can take input from any supported operating system platform. FastLoad can even read the output data directly from a FastExport job, using named pipes, without ever landing the data on a storage device.

FastLoad's speed advantage comes from its ability to leverage Teradata's parallel processing capabilities. Rather than loading in a row-by-row fashion, FastLoad loads data in 64K blocks in parallel per AMP.

However, FastLoad can only be used to load empty tables, and can only insert data; select/update/delete operations are not allowed, and can only operate on a single table. FastLoad is also a very system-intensive process, and only a limited number of FastLoad scripts can run on a Teradata system at a given time. Lastly, FastLoad is typically used to load an empty staging table that will be utilized to INSERT-SELECT into a populated table.

FastExport

FastExport is a high performance data extraction utility. FastExport is the utility of choice when extracting a large volume of data. FastExport excels at creating flat files but can also be used to provide the input data to a FastLoad job, using named pipes, without ever landing the data on a storage device.

FastExport retrieves the data specified from the user's SELECT statement, which is required in the FastExport script. FastExport can retrieve data from multiple tables, via the SELECT statement, and outputs the data into a flat file.

The speed advantage from FastExport comes from its ability to leverage Teradata's parallel processing capabilities. On each AMP, retrieved data is first stored in Spool Space and then sorted. Data is translated into 64K blocks, placed into the correct sequence, and returned to the client. FastExport's ability to return data in 64 blocks, as opposed to returning data in a row-by-row fashion, allows it to extract large amounts of data in a timely manner.

MultiLoad

MultiLoad is an extremely flexible and high-performance load utility that can be used for large volumes of data. Unlike FastLoad, MultiLoad can be used to update, upsert, or delete data from a table, as well as insert data. MultiLoad can work with up to five tables in the same job and each table can have up to twenty different inserts, updates, or deletes performed.

MultiLoad operates at the 64K block level. Data can be updated, inserted, upserted or even deleted. A minor drawback to MultiLoad is that the scripts are not as easy to create as a FastLoad or BTEQ script. MultiLoad is very powerful and great care should be exercised when designing a script.

TPump

Teradata Parallel Data Pump (TPump) is a utility that is specifically designed to handle near real-time updates to Teradata. TPump can be used to insert, update, upsert, or delete data from a table. Like the other load utilities, TPump leverages Teradata's parallel processing architecture. TPump is most often used for small batches of updates, rather than large quantities.

TPump is a popular choice when on demand data processing is required because it has the ability to throttle data (the statement rate) to accommodate system throughput at peak and latent times. The statement rate can be changed within the TPump utility window and later decreased as users log on and for ad-hoc queries.

Teradata Parallel Transporter

Teradata Parallel Transporter (TPT) is unlike other utilities in that it operates as a multiple function load environment. TPT is a consolidated interface that leverages the Teradata parallel INSERTER/SELECTOR/LOAD/UPDATE/EXPORT/STREAM/ODBC operators, which utilizes FastLoad, MultiLoad, FastExport, and TPump underneath the covers. TPT focuses on the entire ETL process, rather than on just one subset. The concept behind TPT is to provide a user with the ability to perform an entire ETL task via a single unified job.

Because TPT utilizes the other utilities, the same rules and restrictions apply. The benefit from using TPT arises from its ability to consolidate an entire ETL process. This leads to easy maintenance, since many tasks are now contained in a single job. TPT also has an open API that allows 3rd party and in-house tools to communicate with Teradata.

Archive and Recovery

The Archive and Recovery (ARC, but often referred to as ARCMAIN) utility is used to backup and restore database and table objects, as well as to recover tables. ARC scripts can either be executed manually at the command line, or implemented with network attached tools. ARC allows for the following operations:

- Archive - ARC allows the archiving of data to physical storage, such as a tape device for an entire database or individual tables. Archiving can be utilized in two ways:

  - Channel-Attached (mainframe) - ARC is used to back up and restore data with Job Control Language (JCL) commands. ARC will backup data directly into the mainframe-attached tape subsystem.

  - Network-Attached - Third-party tape management products utilize ARC to back up data.

- Restore - ARC can restore an entire database or individual table(s) from a backup. Restore is most importantly used in the event of a system failure, such as an AMP failure. There are several scenarios where restoring objects from a backup may be necessary:

  - Non-Fallback tables after a disk failure.
  - Tables that have been corrupted.
  - Tables, views, or macros that have been accidentally dropped.
  - Problems resulting in damaged or lost database objects.
  - Archive a single partition.

- Copy - Similar to a restore, but the copy does not have to be placed onto the same system where the data originated. The copy operation is often used to create copies of a table and/or database onto another system.

- Recovery - For tables that are utilizing the journal options, recovery allows for the rollback and rollforward of data. Journals can be check pointed with a synchronization point and selected journal portions can be deleted.

Teradata Analyst Pack

Teradata Analyst Pack is a suite of tools consisting of the following:

- Teradata Visual Explain
- Teradata System Emulation Tool (TSET)
- Index Wizard
- Statistics Wizard

Below is an overview of the features and functions of each tool.

Teradata Visual Explain

Teradata Visual Explain provides the ability to capture and present the steps of a plan through a graphical user interface (GUI). This tool can provide improved insight and understanding of the Teradata Database Optimizer plan for a given SQL statement. Visual Explain also has the capability to perform comparisons of two or more SQL plans.

In order to provide a query plan, the Teradata Visual Explain tool retrieves the following:

- Database object definitions
- Data demographics
- Cost and cardinality estimates

The information gathered above can assists users in identifying the performance implications such as data skew, stale, or missing statistics.

Lastly, Visual Explain uses the Query Capture Database (QCD) to store query plans. This data can also be used by other Teradata Analyst Pack tools.

Teradata System Emulation Tool (TSET)

Teradata System Emulation Tool (TSET) provides the ability to emulate a production system by gathering all the necessary information in order to simulate the Optimizer process on another Teradata system (i.e. test). This information is used to generate query plans as well as simulate potential Optimizer related issues on a non-production system.

TSET also captures the following:

- System cost parameters
- Object definitions
- Random AMP samples
- Statistics
- Query execution plans
- Demographics

This tool also retrieves information by database, query, or workload. However, it does not export user data.

Index Wizard

Teradata Index Wizard is a graphical user interface (GUI) tool that provides an automated process for improving performance through the use of indexes on a particular workload. This tool guides the user through a step-by-step process by analyzing a database workload, and then offering suggestions for improving query performance. In addition, Index Wizard now has support for Partitioned Primary Indexes (PPI) along with offering recommendations for secondary indexes within a workload.

Statistics Wizard

Teradata Statistics Wizard is a graphical user tool (GUI), which enables users to analyze and automate the collection and re-collection of statistics. The end result of this process is better query plans and performance. Statistics Wizard is primarily utilized for the following:

- Provide recommendations to improve the query performance on a particular workload.
- Enables users to collect, or re-collect statistics on tables, indexes, or columns.
- Schedule the COLLECT STATISTICS activity.

In addition, Statistics Wizard can identify changes and provide recommendations on which tables should have statistics collected. This is based on the following:

- Data and table growth
- Columns and Indexes that would benefit from having statistics collected
- Recommend statistics for a specific workload

This tool also offers users the ability to accept or reject these recommendations.

Teradata Administrator

Teradata Administrator provides a comprehensive Windows-based graphical interface to the Teradata Database Data Dictionary for performing a multitude of database administration tasks on the Teradata Database.

The following functions can be performed:

- Create, Modify and Drop Databases, Users, Roles, Profiles, and User-Defined Types
- Create Tables (using ANSI or Teradata syntax)
- Grant or Revoke access and system rights
- Copy Table, View or Macro definitions to another database, or to another system
- Drop or Rename Tables, Views or Macros
- Move space from one database to another
- Run an SQL query
- Display information about a Database or Users
- Display information about a Table, View or Macro
- Set up the rules for Query and Access Logging

Teradata Administrator keeps a record of all the actions that are taken and can optionally save this record to a file. This record contains a time stamp together with the SQL that is executed, and other information such as the statement's success or failure.

Chapter 9: Practice Questions

1. Which utility loads data in 64K blocks?
    A. BTEQ
    B. FastExport
    C. FastLoad
    D. MultiLoad
    E. TPump

2. Which load utility can have its statement rate dynamically changed to accommodate peak and latent times?
    A. BTEQ
    B. FastExport
    C. FastLoad
    D. MultiLoad
    E. TPump

3. Which of the following utilities is not utilized by TPT?
    A. BTEQ Interactive Mode
    B. FastExport
    C. FastLoad
    D. MultiLoad
    E. TPump

4. To place archived data onto a different system, which option would be used?
    A. Archive
    B. Copy
    C. Recovery
    D. Restore

5. Which Teradata Analyst Pack tool provides feedback at the workload level?
    A. TSET
    B. Index Wizard
    C. Visual Explain
    D. Statistics Wizard

Chapter Notes

Utilize this space for notes, key points to remember, diagrams, areas of further study, etc.

_____

_____

_____

_____

_____

_____

_____

_____

_____

_____

_____

_____

_____

_____

_____

_____

_____

_____

_____

_____

_____

_____

Chapter 10: Workload Management

Certification Objectives

- ✓ Identify the features and functions of the administering and monitoring tools available within the Teradata product suite.
- ✓ Describe the characteristics of work types that Teradata supports.
- ✓ List the purposes of workload management.
- ✓ Describe the characteristics of response time vs. throughput.

Before You Begin

You should be familiar with the following terms and concepts.

Terms	Key Concepts
Workload Management Tools	ViewPoint
Workload Analysis	DBQL, Teradata Workload Analyzer
Teradata Active System Management (TASM)	Creating, managing, and designing workload definitions

Response Time and Throughput

Response time can be defined as the amount of time elapsed between the beginning and the termination of an event, such as a query on a system. It is ideal to have the shortest possible response time. A short response time guarantees that results can be quickly returned to the requestor, enabling a faster decision to be made, based upon the returned data.

Throughput is a measure of how many concurrent tasks or transactions can be completed, per unit of time. In order for a system to operate efficiently, it must be able to work on multiple requests at the same time. Otherwise, bottlenecks will occur, resulting in degraded system performance.

Teradata systems are designed for both optimal response time and throughput performance. Multiple queries can be processed, simultaneously (throughput), and the results are returned in the shortest amount of time possible (response time). If response time and throughput begin to degrade on a Teradata system, you can improve the performance by adding nodes, enabling workload management, or by decreasing the number of concurrent system requests.

Teradata Active System Management

Teradata Active System Management (TASM) is a portfolio of products designed for the analysis, organization and control of workloads inside the Teradata system. It includes system tables and logs, which interact with each other and a common data source. It facilitates automation in the following four key areas of system management:

- Workload management
- Performance tuning
- Capacity planning
- Performance monitoring

TASM allows you to perform the following:

- Limit user concurrent access
- Monitor Service Level Goals (SLGs)
- Determine the workload on a system

- Prioritize and optimize mixed workloads
- Block or Reject user queries based on table access
- Provide consistent response times
- React to hardware failures

These rules include filters, throttles, and "workload definitions". TASM is an enhanced compilation of two core products consisting of the following:

- Viewpoint Workload Designer– Manages and monitors workload strategies
- Teradata Workload Analyzer (TWA) – Analyzes and recommends candidate workloads

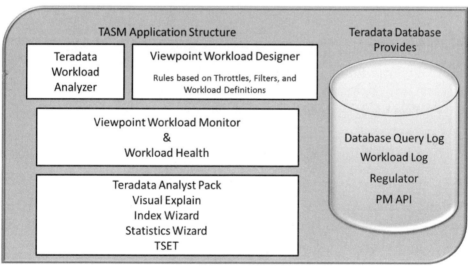

Figure 10.1

Note: Viewpoint is required for workload management on SLES 11, as shown in Figure 10.3.

When utilized together, these tools can monitor workloads in real time along with providing historical reports based on resource utilization by workload. By analyzing this detailed information, workload definitions can be modified to improve query performance, and resource allocations.

Teradata Workload Analyzer

Teradata Workload Analyzer utilizes DBQL data and current Priority Scheduler settings to analyze and identify classes of queries. From there, it can recommend workload strategies as outlined below:

- Offer workload allocation group recommendations and Priority Scheduler Facility (PSF) weight settings.

- Convert Priority Schedule Definitions (PD Sets) into new workloads.

- Recommend appropriate workload Service Level Goals (SLGs) and candidate workloads for analysis.

- Provide workload definitions directly from query history.

- Can be utilized to analyze, measure, and understand existing workload strategies and modify where necessary.

Note: Teradata Workload Analyzer can also apply best practices to workload definitions based on recommendations from Service Level Goal (SLG) objectives and priority scheduler settings.

Teradata Viewpoint

Teradata Viewpoint is a completely new approach to delivering systems management tools and self-service capabilities. Instead of a disparate set of desktop programs, it provides clients with a consistent suite of Web-based applications that can be customized to suit the role of each individual end user. It's an integrated drop-in appliance with a Web-based user interface that can monitor multiple Teradata Database systems, as shown in Figure 11.3. Teradata Viewpoint delivers useful and actionable monitoring and management information to DBAs, managers, and end users.

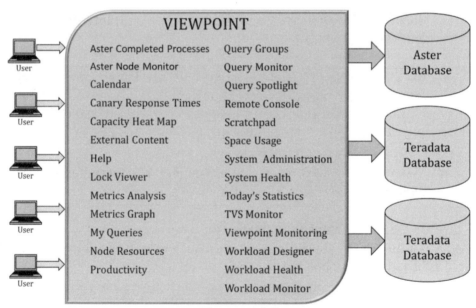

Figure 10.2

The Viewpoint Server is the hardware platform on which the solution stack is installed. It is an Ethernet connected server housed in the Teradata rack and managed by your Administration Workstation and Server Management software.

Teradata Viewpoint consists of a library of portlets that provides both a current view of the workload and throughput of Teradata systems and a historical view of system capacity and use.

- **Teradata Self-Service Portlets**
  These allow users to quickly check system status and performance as well as specific query sessions.

- **Teradata Management Portlets**
  With these, you can monitor the health and current status of Teradata systems and in-flight queries.

- **Teradata Workload Management Portlets**
  Authorized users can monitor and manage mixed workloads running on a Teradata system.

- **Teradata Multi-System Management Portlets**
  Use these portlets to monitor the Teradata Ecosystem's health and the application's components, processes, and tables.

- **Teradata Data Lab Portlets**
  These are used to manage and provision workspace within the Teradata Database.

- **Teradata Data Mover Portlets**
  These portlets monitor and manage data movement between Teradata Databases.

Note: Viewpoint is required for Workload Manager for TD1310 and above and SLES11.

Priority Scheduler

Priority Scheduler is a resource management tool that controls the resource allocation (i.e. CPU) in a Teradata Database system. Priority

Scheduler uses client based requirements and along with system parameters that determine the current activity level of the Teradata Database system. This functionality provides the following:

- Resource and Query Management
- Manage and control the level of resources allocated based on different priorities of queries executing work
- Assigns resources to users
- Enables you to define a prioritized weighting system based on user logon characteristics.
- Balances the workload in your data warehouse based on this weighting system.

Note: Teradata 14.0 TASM includes a new Priority Scheduler design for SLES11. The old Priority Scheduler is an application for TD 14.0 SLES10.

Note: The SLG Responsive Priority Scheduler for SLES11 is based on constructs such as Virtual Partitions, Workload Methods, Access Levels, and Tiers.

Database Query Log (DBQL)

The Database Query Log (DBQL) provides the ability to store historical records of queries such as duration, performance, query counts, and response times that can be charted and used for analysis. In addition, the SQL and processing steps can be compared in order to fine-tune queries for optimum performance. Lastly, DBQL can be customized to log information based on the user or query requests ranging from short transactions to longer-running analysis and data mining.

The Teradata Administrator Tool provides a GUI to configure Query Logging as shown in Figure 10.1:

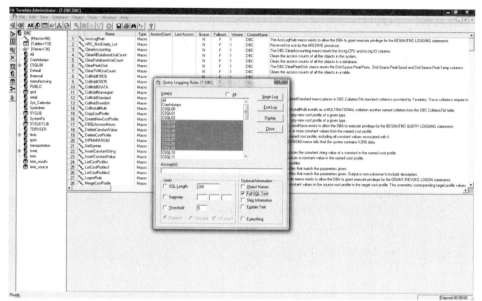

Figure 10.3

To access this interface, from Teradata Administrator, got to Tools >
Query Logging

Chapter 10: Practice Questions

1. Which task is not performed by Teradata Viewpoint?
   A. Monitor system utilization
   B. Define workloads
   C. Assign priorities
   D. Capture query history

2. Which product is not included within Teradata Active System Management (TASM)?
   A. Teradata Workload Analyzer
   B. Teradata SQL Assistant
   C. Database Query Log
   D. Teradata Dynamic Workload Manager

3. Which facility provides a GUI to configure DBQL?
   A. Teradata Workload Analyzer
   B. Teradata SQL Assistant
   C. Teradata Administrator
   D. Teradata Dynamic Workload Manager

4. Which of the following is not included in the Teradata Analyst Pack?
   A. Visual Explain
   B. Index Wizard
   C. TSET
   D. TASM

5. Which product allows you to run, suspend, schedule, or reject queries based on current workload and thresholds?
   A. TSET
   B. TDWM
   C. TDWA
   D. DBQL

Chapter Notes

Utilize this space for notes, key points to remember, diagrams, areas of further study, etc.

_____

_____

_____

_____

_____

_____

_____

_____

_____

_____

_____

_____

_____

_____

_____

_____

_____

_____

_____

_____

_____

_____

_____

_____

Chapter 11: System Management

Certification Objectives

- ✓ Identify the features and use of Unity.
- ✓ Identify the features and use of Data Mover.

Before You Begin

You should be familiar with the following terms and concepts.

Terms	Key Concepts
Components	*Components* are servers that run Teradata Database systems, Teradata Query Director, Teradata Unity, applications, BI, ETL, and replication services.
Processes	Process resources describe data-changing operations.
Data Synchronization	Keeping mission critical information properly mirrored on different systems.

Dual Active Solutions

Dual active uses the second system actively, allowing no idle resources, like in traditional active/standby or disaster recovery solutions. The second active system also provides workload balancing.

Dual Active Solutions allows you to be selective about the data you duplicate, protecting only mission-critical data and applications, while less critical information and applications can be backed up from tape. Dual Active Solutions also allows you more control over which users you route to each system, ensuring that business-critical work receives priority and experiences no downtime.

Teradata Data Mover

Teradata Data Mover (DM) enables you to define jobs that copy specified database objects, such as tables, users, views, macros, stored procedures, and statistics, from one Teradata Database system to another.

In addition to tables and statistics, the following database objects associated with tables can be copied with the tables, but not by themselves:

- Hash indexes
- Join indexes
- Journals
- Triggers

Dual-active support of active copying between two systems is provided through the graphic, command-line, and table-driven interfaces of Teradata DM, which allows you to:

- Establish systems to enable copying, or recover systems to re-enable copying
- Copy a large volume of data from one Teradata Database system to another on a regularly-scheduled basis
- Perform a partial copy of tables from a source Teradata Database system to a target system

In the command-line interface, you can use commands to define jobs, use jobs, and set up and start the table-driven interface. If Teradata Viewpoint is installed in your environment, you can access the functionality of Teradata DM in a user-friendly graphic interface.

If Teradata Multi-System Manager (MSM) is installed in your environment, it can be used to monitor and control Teradata DM.

Teradata Multi-System Manager

Teradata Multi-System Manager (Teradata MSM) intelligently monitors dual system performance and, through Teradata Query Director, acts where necessary to ensure high availability and failover protection.

For example, Teradata MSM can detect that System A is experiencing a slowdown and data currency is not keeping up with System B. Teradata MSM then does the following:

- Determines which users and applications are affected.
- Determines which users among those affected have mission-critical applications.
- Communicates with Teradata Query Director, which routes those users and their data to System B.

Teradata Multi-System Manager also monitors the data synchronization status between the two systems and integrates with Teradata Replication Services.

Teradata Query Director

Teradata Query Director routes queries between dual active systems for load balancing and failover based on rules you set up in advance, for example:

- Marketing users are normally routed to System A, which gives them an average 2 second response time.
- Finance users are normally routed to System B, which gives them an average 5 second response time.
- If System A is down, all users are transparently and automatically routed to System B, with Marketing users receiving processing priority. Marketing users still see 2

second response times, while Finance users may see 30 second response times. Users do not have to log in to the other system and do not notice the rerouting.

Teradata Replication Services

Teradata Replication Services is optimal when:

- Data is updated on the source system with SQL by interactive or other non-batch applications.
- The batch job or transaction size is moderate (10,000 rows or fewer).
- It is important to minimize the lag time in updates between two Teradata systems.

Data Synchronization Method	Recommended Use
Table Copy (Data Mover)	Copy complete tables (or partial tables based on a timestamp or batch number) from one system to another on an automated periodic schedule.
Dual Load	Load large amounts of data external to the Teradata systems onto both Teradata systems at once.
Replication	Replicate moderate-sized changes from SQL transactions from one Teradata system to another in real-time.

Figure 11.1

Note: Replication Services uses Golden Gate for Oracle to Teradata replication. Teradata to Teradata replication uses Unity Data Mover.

Teradata Unity

Teradata Unity provides a data virtualization layer that enables you to maintain fully active independent Teradata Database servers for continuous availability and horizontal scalability.

Teradata Unity, which is deployed on two Teradata Managed Servers (TMS) for high availability, virtualizes Teradata Database servers under its control so that applications are not aware that there are multiple database servers. To the applications, the Teradata Unity server is the database.

Each database server in the Teradata Unity environment maintains its own data. Teradata Unity does not store any data on its own server, except for recovery purposes. The feature distributes the SQL requests from applications to the appropriate Teradata Database servers, as required.

The latest release of Unity brings additional capabilities, an enhanced level of integration between the products in the Teradata Unity portfolio and new names, as shown in the following chart Figure 11.2.

Function	Previous Product name	New Product name
End-to-end monitoring and control	Teradata Multi-System Manager	Unity Ecosystem Manager
Data synchronization, user and query routing	Teradata Query Director Teradata Replication Services	Unity Director
Database synchronization	Teradata Replication Services Dual Load	Unity Loader
Data movement	Teradata Data Mover	Unity Data Mover

Figure 11.2

Unity Ecosystem Manager

For end-to-end monitoring and control, Unity Ecosystem Manager replaces Teradata Multi-System Manager. It monitors dependencies between components, processes and tables, and it allows administrators to set threshold alerts and automated actions to help organizations deliver on service level agreements.

Unity Director

Supporting data and database synchronization, user and query routing, Unity Director uses patented SQL Multicast technology to intelligently and selectively deliver database instructions to all affected Teradata systems. It can automatically route queries between the systems, based on the query's SQL syntax, to create a "plug-and-play" solution without requiring a query routing setup. As the replacement for Teradata Query Director and most functions of Teradata Replication Services, Unity Director can route users' sessions like Query Director did, giving administrators direct control over specific system access.

In the same way that it routes queries based on SQL syntax, Unity Director also maintains data synchronization across systems when SQL update queries are run or when external data updates come through SQL-based load utilities. The queries and updates are intelligently routed and applied to the appropriate systems.

Unity Director has additional functionality that maintains database synchronization across systems by routing and applying data definition language changes to the appropriate systems—greatly reducing the workload for administrators in a multi-system environment.

Data and database updates, which were handled through change data capture (CDC) using Teradata Replication Services, can now be applied directly to the appropriate Teradata systems using Unity Director

Unity Loader

Intelligent data loading is enabled by Unity Loader replacing custom-built "dual load" solutions. It applies the underlying capabilities of SQL Multicast to Teradata Parallel Transporter bulk load utilities—intelligently and selectively routing the loads to the appropriate Teradata system or systems with no additional effort required by administrators. Plus, it replaces a common use of the former Teradata Replication Services in which data is bulk loaded into a table on one system, then copied over to the other systems using CDC.

Unity Data Mover

Teradata Data Mover is replaced by Unity Data Mover for fast and efficient data movement between Teradata systems. It allows administrators to focus on the purpose and intent of the movement rather than the specific utility and syntax being used.

Chapter 11: Practice Questions

1. Which tool is not part of Teradata Unity?
    A. Teradata Administrator
    B. Teradata Data Mover
    C. Teradata Multi-System Manager
    D. Teradata Query Director
    E. Teradata Viewpoint
    F. Teradata Replication Services

2. Which of the following synchronizes data by copying tables from one system to another?
    A. Teradata Administrator
    B. Teradata Data Mover
    C. Teradata Multi-System Manager
    D. Teradata Viewpoint
    E. Teradata Query Director
    F. Teradata Replication Services

3. Which of the following includes the Ecosystem Manager?
    A. Teradata Administrator
    B. Teradata Data Mover
    C. Teradata Multi-System Manager
    D. Teradata Viewpoint
    E. Teradata Unity
    F. Teradata Query Director
    G. Teradata Replication Services

4. Which of the following includes an Aster portlet?
   A. Teradata Administrator
   B. Teradata Data Mover
   C. Teradata Multi-System Manager
   D. Teradata Viewpoint
   E. Teradata Unity
   F. Teradata Query Director
   G. Teradata Replication Services

5. Which of the following synchronizes data by copying transaction changes from one system to another?
   A. Teradata Administrator
   B. Teradata Data Mover
   C. Teradata Multi-System Manager
   D. Teradata Viewpoint
   E. Teradata Query Director
   F. Teradata Replication Services

6. Which tool is used to load large amounts of external data to dual Teradata systems?
   A. Teradata Administrator
   B. Teradata Data Mover I believe this is correct, NOT E
   C. Teradata Multi-System Manager
   D. Teradata Query Director
   E. Teradata Replication Services

7. Which of the following is deployed on two Teradata Managed Servers?
   A. Teradata Administrator
   B. Teradata Data Mover
   C. Teradata Multi-System Manager
   D. Teradata Viewpoint
   E. Teradata Unity
   F. Teradata Query Director
   G. Teradata Replication Services

8. Which of the following is used to manage workloads?
   A. Teradata Administrator
   B. Teradata Data Mover
   C. Teradata Multi-System Manager
   D. Teradata Viewpoint
   E. Teradata Unity
   F. Teradata Query Director
   G. Teradata Replication Services

Chapter Notes

Utilize this space for notes, key points to remember, diagrams, areas of further study, etc.

Teradata 14 Certification Study Guide

Appendix

Answers to Chapter Practice Questions

Chapter 1		Chapter 2		Chapter 3		Chapter 4	
1.	B	1.	A	1.	E	1.	D
2.	D	2.	D	2.	A	2.	C
3.	B	3.	D	3.	B	3.	B
4.	E	4.	B	4.	C	4.	A
5.	F	5.	C	5.	D	5.	E
6.	D	6.	D	6.	A	6.	D
7.	C			7.	A, D		

Chapter 5		Chapter 6		Chapter 7		Chapter 8	
1.	A	1.	E	1.	B	1.	B
2.	F	2.	C	2.	A-3	2.	D
3.	B	3.	A		B-4	3.	B
4.	C	4.	B		C-1	4.	A
5.	A	5.	C		D-2	5.	AD
6.	D			3.	D		
7.	A			4.	B		
8.	A			5.	B		
				6.	C		

Chapter 9		Chapter 10		Chapter 11	
1.	C	1.	D	1.	A
2.	E	2.	B	2.	B
3.	A	3.	C	3.	E
4.	B	4.	D	4.	D
5.	B	5.	B	5.	F
				6.	E
				7.	E
				8.	D

Index